DEDICATION

To the eternal children who struggle with the magnificent nature of their physical confines, ego and polarity tissues used to make up the fear in our brain. Many of us have become slaves to those perpetuating truths and fears. Our potential still yet to be realized because of our distractions with this world. I have faith in humanity's nature. I am confident we will put aside childish distractions and will all stand in awe of each other once again. Or the species will return to our nature and parish without evolving because of our distractions. Either way our nature will win.

May your heart bring you wisdom and love; allowing you to evolve and witness the vampires and zombies in your life, today. May it allow you to demonstrate compassion for them; to find balance with the fear inhabiting your brain. May your heart and mind be balanced enough to walk among them, without becoming so distracted by their childish fears and truths that you join them.

1

CONTENTS

A DEFINING MOMENT

As you read the words on this page you are creating the potential for a defining moment. Right Now! You have the opportunity to think about the world from a different perspective. Maybe this chance is because someone recommended the book to you. You came into contact with this opportunity for some reason. It makes no difference how it happened you can pick either the label of fate or chance. Use an excuse for reading the book, announce it as a revelation, or say it happened by accident; the results are the same. You are here, in your present moment and how you carry it forward makes it 100% your story. The words may have been brought to you in this format, however, you must consider this a defining moment, designed by you.... For example, you can continue to read the words or stop. You may be partially distracted by events of the day which cause you to miss nuances in the sentences or maybe you are immersed in the words not missing a single gem. This investment makes it your moment, you own it and your moment is what you make of it. Hell, maybe you put the book back on the shelf and walk away because your heart knows you are not ready for the experience. It is all by your design. You have these opportunities many times every single day. You are having it regardless of conscious thought as you continue to consume the book pages and think. These defining moments are the magical times where you are listening to yourself and ask questions too difficult for the mind to answer. Questions like "Is this really how you want to live your life?" or "Is this really what life is about?" These are your moments of definition and you can choose to either ignore the distractions of your world and listen to the moment with your heart or turn up the noise in your life and drowned it out of your brain in an effort to remain distracted from those hard questions.

You have now been reading the book for a couple of minutes "consuming" a couple of the basic concepts and questions we all ask ourselves. You have also been creating labels and opinions from the moment you looked at the cover. Is this thought of automatically labelling what you perceive through your eyes interesting to you? Is it interesting that none of these ideas are really new to you, even if you have not heard them expressed in exactly this way before?

This book is designed for the newcomer to the idea of "awakening" to more than what the physical world is able to offer them. When I say "awake" I am not talking about the label used by people to identify themselves as being something that someone else is yet to achieve. When I say awakening I am referring to an individual's awareness of themselves and their state of being self-aware. Being self-aware is no picnic, it is not a joy ride, just a lot of hard work. There is an easy way to determine the difference between those using a label and those on a journey. A key difference I have noted between those who are awake and those who are still distracted by using this label is that those who are truly awake have no idea how much work they still have to do with themselves to consider themselves "awake". So these people find no value saying they are "awake" or "enlightened". However, those distracted by the label of it and who say they are awake still do not grasp the importance of understanding the goal as a journey, not a destination.

When I was at this place of seeking to understand this process I sought out the best and brightest explanations. I ran into many frustrating times because I was seeking the label. The goal; using someone else's method. Then one day sitting in a coffee shop while watching people come in and rush out on their way to their lives I became aware of something. Frustration. I was frustrated by my own lack of comprehension. BUT, here is the tricky part. It was a conscious thought of the emotion, being frustrated, not of the goal to understand. Suddenly the emotion was separate from my goal. I was able to see that the emotion was prompting me to give up and just let the elusive nature of being "awake" be the goal of someone else. I had a courtesy conversation from my ego trying to convince me that I had plenty of other labels (husband, dad, employee, friend, etc.) I was damn good at and could be distracted by those for the rest of my life. I found myself practicing being present in the moment. It was a defining moment for me. I had been working so hard to get from here.....to there. The depressing part was understanding that in that moment that there was no finish line. I also realized a vast majority of people I knew had no idea what I just explained to you. They were too distracted by their smartphones, world events, or any number of physical attractions available to all of us. Here in lies a world of zombies and vampires distracted in an effort to avoid the work involved with being aware/awaken to themselves.

There are also those who believe there is more to themselves than the distractions being offered by the physical world. If this is you, then hopefully you can use something from my experiences and perspectives so that you may experience your own defining moments. Some may look at this as a beginner's guide to being awake. I would offer that the life experiences and understanding the perspective of another person is never a beginning…While I discovered there is no finish line to this journey I also realized that there is no starting line either. We do not all line up at the same place and begin a race on the path to enlightenment. Being awake is a fluid state of being based on your own design, not one found in any one book or taught by any self-proclaimed gurus, but rather in a world of people who are each, themselves, books with experiences which can be helpful to you in your lifetime. It is your own experiences and perspectives bumped up against the insights and realities of others. Those insights may be adopted by you or put back on the shelf… This is all up to you. You define your moment, but we will get to that later.

So then why the book? Well, it was not really my idea, in some ways. I was on my own journey and what I was learning I was also writing down. It organized itself into these thoughts and would not let me sleep at night until I started writing them into the format you are reading today. I would like to think that this effort is designed to help people discover their own path. For them to understand that the path is not hard to find, but can be extremely challenging to stay on over time. Yes, it is exciting to travel and experience new things, but there is struggle and darkness, too. At some point in the journey it leads you to a place you already know exists inside yourself, but have forgotten exists.

Now let's imagine you are going to purchase this book and consume the information, digest it as you feel appropriate, and put into practice based on your perspective of what you have read. Let's say some of the concepts in this book are hard to talk about or your perception was clouded by emotions as you consumed the pages. How will you address those pages? It is these perspectives during these moments that define them for you and your future. Take your time, be patient with yourself and read slowly. It is not those things easy to agree with or those things you already know, but the uncomfortable things that will put you on the path or may cause you to close the book for another day or maybe another lifetime. Reading these pages, buying this book, and influencing other based on how you have perceived what you have digested makes you a consumer. This makes us all consumers. But honestly, that is what we came into this human form to be.

To borrow the concept of humanity from several theologies; we were created in the image and likeness of our source, because we ourselves were a part of that source. We took that perfect-ness and crammed it all into this meat suit of imperfect-ness, that by its very nature, required sustenance be consumed to maintain its' existence. We have to consume liquids and food for the meat suit to survive. This process is not perfect. If it was it would not produce something we call "waste". It would not grow old and would not expire thereby returning our perfectness to its' original state. Understanding this lack of perfect-ness is important later when we discuss balance and Hitler.

So I have chosen to classify the world into three consuming categories. The zombie, the vampire, and those who are awake. Classifying the world into three categories immediately brings the ego into play….Which category of consumer am I? Right? Ok, well put the ego aside for a few minutes and let's review some of the finer points of this journey.

Here is the real question…..Why did this book even catch your eye? Would you have even given it a second glance if it was title "Awakening the Enlightened, Consumer, and Life Sucking Force"? Something about the book appealed to you from the first glance, what about it opened your eyes? So why do you continue reading? You got the main idea, there really can't be that much more in the 100+ pages that are relevant to your current journey and search for life's answers. Can there?

Now a book publisher may say, "Take this part out. You are daring the reader to put it back on the shelf." Well, that is exactly what I am doing. If you have ever told someone they need to "open their eyes" or "wake up" it is because in that time you have the ability to see passed the fear that is gripping them and you know, in your gut, what advice they may need to hear. Now in those times, how often has the person you have giving advice to move in the opposite direction? This is why I say when you are ready you will create your defining moment. What you do with that moment is not for me to decide, but I would like you to come on this journey with me. You may not, consciously, know why you picked up this book, but maybe it is because you are now ready to re-member. Continue reading

6

and it will all start to fit, the idea of a massive group of people who do nothing, except consume everything around them, as a global society of humanity begins to make sense. These are your zombies.

Then there are those people who prey on the zombies energies endlessly, these are the vampires and they feed on all of those who are trying to get out of the dazed drone like state. We will discuss the vampires in more detail shortly. Finally, there is you and me, we are trying so hard to stay awake, or balanced, or enlightened, or whatever it is we are when we see the world around us feeding on its own insanity. Sure we consume as well, but it is this state of consumption that is most interesting because here we are not feeding on anything external to ourselves. We are feeding on the energy of the universe from within ourselves. Stay with me.

This book is designed for those who have awakened a couple of times, but have seen what has been created, decided it was too hard to make a difference and have gone back to sleep. This book is for those who can see the road less travelled but are not sure how to get on it. This book is designed for those who are starting to experience their own brilliance but are scared of it and what the consequences may be. This book is for the awakening. So many times when I started this journey I found books that would "speak to me", however, it was a real struggle to get from here….to there. This is your defining moment; this is your chance to move off the path of least resistance and onto the path of bliss. This is what I want to help you with. I do not mention hour long meditations or yoga because you are just waking up, yet the books I have read in the past move you into a difficult state right from the beginning. I want to ease you into this new state of being. Are you still with me? GREAT!

The saying that "Life imitates art" was something I heard every year when we went on school field trips. In today's age of technology I believe that our social life imitates our music and television. Consider how really scary this is. Look at your 150 + TV channels and identify the emotions you feel with each program. Do this with the evening news first. Next move to prime time TV shows, what emotions are they generating? This really hit me one night as I watched my daughter's expressions while she was watching a show with vampires. They were discussing how they should feed on the humans like "cattle". This prime time TV show was demonstrating

7

the struggle one of the characters was having with their own "humanity" and the look on my daughter's face was one of pain for the character, but at the same time there was an element of jealousy I could sense from her as well. I could see she was fascinated by the speed and abilities of the vampires and jealous of these skills but was sensitive to the desire to be a part of humanity. Isn't this where you are today? How do you fit into the greater whole that is humanity? You want to participate, you want to actively be of service to others, so what stops you? Maybe you feel society is lost? Or is it you who is lost? Is there a difference? Then the TV show breaks to commercial and there is an advertisement for a Zombie Chase activity. This is where people pay to be either chased by zombies OR to be a zombie chasing people from point A to point B. This is all the rage right now and the companies sponsoring these events are making a lot of money. So an opening question to myself might be: Why would I want to be a contributing member of humanity when all I am seeing is a global society of zombies? Fortunately, not everyone is a zombie, there are a lot of vampires, too. And there is you, fluctuating between the two and hoping there is a third option. This is a fear. Do you know where this is rooted? Is it rooted in a desire to know where you belong? This question is something that needs to be identified and released in order to find the bliss in your life. It will be a journey which will feel like a marathon, not a sprint and will be no small task. It might take you years to get to a point where you can learn to ask enough questions to get it all sorted out. Are you sure your still interested in the path of self-awareness? Game consoles and streaming movie services are much easier.... The world is full of people who will tell you where you belong, but will you listen to them? What about yourself? Will you listen to yourself? Where are you listening from? Do you believe you are going to find your awareness by following the logic and polarity of your brain? Where does your heart fit in? When do you do something because it feels right, not just because it makes sense? Maybe you are thinking these are reasonable questions and a good place to start. Excellent! Pick one and start... It is going to be a fun ride!!

This is what I meant when I said you will be given the opportunity to define your moments every single day. Your reality is filled with experiences you will overlook or just miss because you are distracted. You will miss the questions which is even more important

8

than knowing some of those answers. Is it true that we have already identified a vast majority of our humanity as zombies? We live in a society where people stare at their phones every waking moment, have zero tolerance for anyone with a different opinion than them and would just as soon eat their brains as have a healthy debate about the topics creating the conflict. What do you think? This is a good time to tell you that this book is not about giving you answers for your questions. It is the opportunity for you to step into the perspective of my reality. To understand the questions I found important in my journey. If you think I am going to give you your answers, well no one can do that and I have already explained why. Did you catch it when I said it or did you breeze past that paragraph? I said you are a unique expression of one. Anyone else who tells you they know what your answers are, is full of shit!

In my reality the masses of humanity have been stupefied by technology and wander through their lives like zombies. During their wanderings they are fed on by their bosses, who are fed on by their bosses, all the way up to the corporate leaders of the world. You are a unique expression of one. It may be dulled at times by zombie vision or you may be tired after the vampire feeding frenzy, but you are still one… Somewhere inside you understand this fact, you can relate to it and you want to understand more about it.

Vampires are extremely popular on TV and in theaters right now. They are not only represented metaphorically in the social, political, and economic machines controlled in schools and businesses around the world but can also be represented by individuals who have learned how to feed on the lives of others. Unfortunately for us and the zombies, none of these vampires sparkle or have fangs. Unlike the zombies, a vampire does not rely on big groups for strength. They have mastered how to survive among all the zombies by leading them. You may consider a vampire a step up one level in the re-evolutionary chain, but they are missing something they crave and are just like everyone else who is unique... Except they think they will find it through power and the ability to control things. Yet they have not found it, this thing they seek is still out there.

As in the movies, their thirst is unquenchable and it is not for your blood, but for something far more precious to you. In our world, nothing exists without energy. The universe runs on it and our physical forms rely on it, but in our social world, it is the energy surrounded by having a certain level of status or significance. The

9

vampire tries to quench this thirst through something we know as "power". By significance or power I mean being popular, wealthy, or anything that brings about a separation from others through a label or status. Isn't it ironic that we have taken a physical form to understand the feeling of being unique and creating a separation from the source, but that was not enough for us. We now strive in our human existence for labels of significance to further separate ourselves from each other. We then spend our precious time in this physical reality trying to find our way back to the source, where we will end up when we die. Does this sound like a waste of time to anyone else? We do this through a variety of methods, but in the process miss those opportunities for our defining moments. When we are given the opportunity to understand or appreciate these moments, for some zombies, it is to hard so we deny or distract ourselves from understanding any more about it...Or ourselves. Many of us then add insult to injury by refusing to be accepting of how others have learned to relate to that energy, the bliss they enjoy, or the freedom they seem to have found. Zombies get jealous.

It may seem really bizarre talking about these two fictitious character types, but are they really fictitious? Are movies just imitating what we are seeing people do in their daily lives? Or can everything I said above be summed up by just saying "Life's a bitch and then you die."

We walk through this human experience, but do we really find joy or follow our bliss? In our day-to-day lives we spend a good portion of it sleeping, eating, and enjoying leisure activities as time permits. A majority of us spend the remainder of our time doing what other people demand from us, socially, which includes working for others to bring them power and buying things to sustain ourselves and give power to others. Our final priority, if we are not too tired, may result in doing what we truly enjoy. Our governments, corporations, and even social structures rely on the ability to drain your energy to stay alive. Vampires.

As a result many of us wander through life as a zombie. Those "stuck in their ways" are those that are the most asleep. Many of them do not want to be disturbed. My advice, leave them alone. You need to understand yourself and if you try to wake them by making statements or quoting facts to them, they will seek your destruction. I have seen this destruction occur in three general ways. If you ask

10

someone close to you questions which awaken them, the first thing you will witness is the horde. The horde are all of their friends with similar beliefs. They will use this horde to rally strength and energy to deflect your statements, questions and even your facts. You will be going on a journey with them and as a unique expression of One, you will be alone. The hordes goal is to destroy your state of curiosity and to bring you back into the horde. You are their friend, their family, even their strength and they cannot allow you to make them think. The second method I have seen is if the person you are speaking to is not strong enough to deflect your theories one on one or they do not have a horde they can lean on to defend them. In this situation you may witness a complete shutdown of communication and they may avoid being around you at all costs. When confronted with the opportunity to wake up they may choose instead to hide from it…and you. You will be ignored, which in many cases is the best case scenario for you. While both of those situations sound bad I think the worst case I have experienced is a one-on-one exchange which on the surface seems to be going well, until it is not. The person you are sharing with suddenly lashes out and becomes angry or irrational in the conversation. I see these events as allergic reactions. What you are saying takes some time before it disturbs their inner sleep. Once it does, you see the results of waking them up and results will vary.

Be mindful that this is a painful process and you have chosen it for you, but not everyone wants it in their reality. It is not your job to tell people how they should live in this short lifespan any more than it is their job to limit you from finding your own bliss.

You cannot help or save anyone who wants to remain asleep. You cannot convince vampires not to feed on them in pursuit of their own power. You can only seek your own understanding of your unique expression of one. Period. The benefits to this journey will include meeting others along the way who wish to understand your journey and will appreciate your perspective. Those who understand themselves and are open to understanding others are closer to source because they understand and can relate to what it is you are seeking in your own journey. They appear when you need them, sometimes for a moment…other times for a lifetime.

This is why I anticipate my book being valued by very few and probably ignored by the masses. Remember this is not only outside your extended circle of friends, but this also extends everywhere in your life, not just those who are the coworkers and drones in the workplace....Think about family members who are theology zealots, those who wave a political banner and yes even die-hard sports fans. These are zombies, in a horde, common in a belief and they have all the answers. They strive to make everyone around them a part of their horde. They want everyone else to be as irritated or excited as they are about their faith, the political state of things or the fact that "their" team went to the championship game. Zombies need stability and consistency from those around them, so asking questions or making statements which disturb the stability may result in you not getting invited to next year's Super Bowl party.... Those people have already lost interest in reading this book, because it irritates them or makes them uncomfortable. I would anticipate parts of this book will do the same to you, but you are not here to have your perspective reinforced are you? You are here to consider the magical nature of yourself, to explore the world through the perspective of others. So if you are still with me, congratulations....you are not a zombie.....All the time. What does that mean? All the time? Well, if I am self-aware and I enjoy meeting with like minded people who share similar views am I not a part of a horde? When I go to a family dinner and remain silent about things I am passionate about around others, am I not pretending to be a part of a horde? Tough questions, right. We have a lot more questions to go before you find those answers which will be meaningful to you.

Again, I am not trying to tell you how to experience your unique nature. I honor that your magnificent being has the right to experience it in any number of ways. Instead, I hope to share with you how many ways are possible based on my own experiences and perspective. The more of these you can expose yourself too, the richer your experience in the defining moments, your present moment, and your entire lifetime.

At this point in the book, you are on a bicycle and peddling towards a very steep downward hill, right now there is a lot of peddling involved to get you to the crest of this hill and you are moving under your own power at your own speed. If you pedal faster and speed through this book you may miss the meaning behind the words and when you head down the hill you may find yourself off in the dirt as a result of not properly preparing yourself for this ride. It is easy to read words, but the comprehension of the sentence takes many moments more for yourself to absorb and process. Add more time to process these questions if my words cause you to be emotional. If you feel emotional then put the book aside and allow yourself to be in that space with that question which has triggered the emotion. Emotions are great, however, if you read and carry emotions at the same time then the opportunity for the defining moment in your heart will take several moments or may be missed all together. As you are peddling and getting closer to this hill I would recommend taking it slow and ensure you comprehend the words as they are placed in the sentences. Soon you will be racing down this hill with no need to peddle only to hold on as you read. It will be at this time you will be glad you took the journey to the crest of the hill, slow. The point, take your time.

Consider that every child born is a vampire. The child MUST rely on others to feed them both physically and energetically. Studies have been conducted showing that a child without human contact will cease to exist. It has been shown that people who feel disconnected from humanity can use their own will to cease existing. The younger the person, the easier it seems to just stop participating in humanity. They know how to starve themselves to death energetically and give up physically. So, consider the needs of a newborn child, they will not survive for very long without the influence and interaction of those around them. When a parent holds a newborn child for the first time there is a connection that is created between those two, this connection is not something that you can see or even that a parent can define, but it is there. Holding my newborn daughter for the first time opened an emotional part in me that I cannot describe in words, but it moved me instantly and I have seen other new parents affected the same way. This was not because of the physical contact; it was something I did not understand at the time. Part of this experience is a way for the child to feed off of the energy and love provided by the parent. This energy is provided freely by the parent and is often equated to an emotion, but rarely thought of solely as an energy connection. If every child begins as a vampire then as they get older they have the potential to grow and evolve into much more, or the alternative is to not grow and evolve by becoming a zombie. It is the parents who may first influence the direction, but the children have an innate compass they can follow as well. This is especially true of those children who have been classified as "indigo" or "rainbow" children,

13

but in this case these children have the ability to listen and follow that internal self much easier and learn quickly how to be more than just a vampire.

It is ironic that while writing this book several things have become reality. There is a motion picture soon to be released titled "Warm Bodies" that applies a comical nature to the same principles I have written in this book. I am excited for this movie to be released so I can see just how close it is to a reality based in love. The trailer of the movie made it apparent that it was when the zombie began to "feel", that they begin to wake up. This is not far off of the premise of this book. The main question is how do we get all the zombies to start feeling?

How many Halloween costumes did you see this year that were either a vampire or a zombie? I saw a lot of them. What is the fascination?

I am not the only one who lives in this world, you know and work with many people who you are able to identify as a zombie or vampire now, also. Some of these people may be a part of your immediate family and you have seen this throughout your childhood. For those of us who grew up as part of a large family you can remember when there were an odd number of siblings in the house. It was usually two against one for everything from where the family would eat when eating out, to arguments about which games to play on the weekends. The mob mentality of the zombies starts very early in our lives and today we refer to them as gangs. We learned early on that by being part of the gang we were much stronger. So we wanted friends around us all the time to keep us strong and we would do anything for them, no matter what the cost.

I use the word "gangs" and you may think I am referring to street gangs or drug gangs based on TV shows. No, here I am referring to the society gangs and our cultural gangs that act as a group and label you as either "in" or "out". With the zombies it is easy to identify them because of their group mentality and desire to consume things immediately. This consumption can happen through the use of technology, political views, taught theology's, and the energy individuals seem to hoard as part of a group when attacking or "dog piling" on other groups. Many times these people, when by themselves, will be relatively quiet, however, when they are with others who support their views their voice and energy seem to grow because they are empowered by the energy of the horde, if you are

14

around them for any length of time you will sense this energy and may even desire to be a part of it.

When I refer to "feeding" I am referring to an energy drain or pull which makes you feel tired. You get this when around vampires. A child will do this to their parents with relative ease and if the parents are not aware of how to recharge themselves, well they are "exhausted" by the end of the day even if they did not do any physical activity. A zombie horde is different because it shares energy within a group. This horde feeds on the energy being generated by the group, some refer to this type of energy and the resulting activities as being a mob mentality. So now consider a prayer circle. Zombie or Vampire? Too soon? Ok, let's keep moving. For those needing a nap after a football game or a parent who just needs a quick nap while their child is sleeping. It is at those times that the body restores the energy you freely shared. Your energy levels can quickly be restored when your conscious mind is out of the way. This is also why when getting up in the morning we feel "refreshed". Your body has had a chance to reenergize and recover from the zombies and vampires in your life.

First let's define a zombie culture. These are the people who are a product of their society but are void of thought outside of what they are told to think. Think about this for a moment. All zombies and vampires rely on mass media to form their opinion for them. A zombie's opening line in conversations start with statements like: "Did you hear what (fill in political, news or religious leader here) said yesterday on TV?"….OR a statement may start with "I just do my job and keep my head down." How about "I do it that way because that is the way I was taught to do it" or "My team is going to the championship game!". These are just a couple of zombie statements and this is the state of walking through life as a zombie. Go to a major sporting event, look at all the $40 jerseys people are wearing to support their favorite team. Mob mentality feeds off of the team's victories….and defeats with either positive or negative emotion. Zombies have been conditioned for life by the education system, been force fed it through television, and is reinforced for them in the workplace by other zombies and their vampire bosses. If you want a different perspective on this, take the day off; go to the coffee shop at 7 am. Get a coffee and watch the 7:30am zombie parade….just watch as the day to day life starts for many people and they come in and get their coffee, look at their watch absent-

15

mindedly, and wander back out to their car. I have seen people look at their watch or phone no less than four times while standing in line for two minutes. They are doing it out of reflex and they have been conditioned to make sure they are connected to the clock or their job in some way, constantly. Want to verify it is reflex? Wait until you see someone look at their watch, wait 30 seconds and ask them what time it is. A thought conscious person will tell you the time and a zombie will look at their watch again. This is because it has become their lifeline to their world, it is the same reason they will look at their phone during meals and on weekends if only for 60 seconds to ensure they are connected.

After the zombie parade has slowed at the coffee shop go over to the neighborhood mall, watch the people who are out in the mid-morning....They are not much better and most of them are on a mission to get something and get on to the next thing on their list. People are most all moving with purpose and are frustrated when they cross paths with those who are not in a hurry. Now it is lunch time, stop and have lunch in a food court or popular restaurant. What do you see? Zombies and Vampires.

Zombies are never by themselves; they move in groups and feel lost without being a part of a larger group. The vampires do not mind being alone in public, but are normally so distracted by business conversations that they do not notice the world around them. If you do happen to catch a person alone they usually have another soul on the phone with them while they hurry through their tasks. These are your zombies and vampires in a relaxed state of consumption. Need an example? When was the last time you ate a meal alone, with no, electronic leash, (phone)? When was the last time you went to see a movie, in a theater, alone? What stigma does going to a movie alone carry for you? "I just don't like being alone" is a typical zombie response. What does that statement really mean? Have you ever taken the time to really look at it and ask yourself the question? Is it a question of safety? Consider, as long as everyone consumes right along with them, according to society expectations, they will be safe. Is this the safety you seek?

Let's experiment with that thought, next, go to a park or a playground where there are young children and watch how they interact with each other. You will notice that many of the children play together, but also have no issue with playing alone. The children are generally happy and are moving about the playground

16

without much concern of what is happening in the world around them. Look around the park at the other people and their activities. How does this compare to what you saw earlier? How does the energy level differ? Now, include yourself in the world of a parents society and sit with other parents on a bench close to the children and watch them explore their world. Observant parents who saw you come alone will begin to question your motives for being there and you can feel their energy shift. Better yet, release your inner child and approach a child, sit in the sand and play with them….How long do you think it will be until the parental society confronts you directly or calls in a police officer to discuss your behavior with you? Do you now believe this could become physical? You stopped being a zombie and wanted to play with the other children who were following their bliss. Unfortunately, many parents do not remember theirs either, so you have a problem. You got the other zombies attention, still question how safe it is?

The vampire is altogether different. While there are groups of vampire "covens" that feed on the masses they, unlike the zombies, do not have to run in packs to drain someone's energy and often times are very comfortable feeding on the masses by themselves. These "covens" are institutions which will likely include big businesses and governments, but I did not have to tell you that, you already knew this…..Didn't you? Conversations with the vampire will normally begin with statements like "that is just the way the world is" or "you can't beat the system" and my favorite "You get what you pay for". The vampire mentality is one of strategy and meticulous thought usually similar to a game of chess. They seek out and drain the energy from those with idealistic or independent thought, first. Those who are spirited, have integrity, and want to make a difference, vibrate at a much higher level than those who only have self-interests. This is often seen in day to day life as they feed off of another person's success or tragedy with the equal eagerness. They will feed on the zombies, but get much more of a charge out of feeding off of independent thought and free spirited people. They will surround themselves with those like them, but who, they believe, they are strategically superior to or can easily control. They like to use phrases like "keep your friends close, and your enemies closer." Or "to the victor go the spoils." They are always looking at all the angles and always finding ways to help others see things their way. The primary target of a vampire are

17

those who show "promise" and they often offer to act as a mentor to the individual, but are strategic enough to see a benefit in this mentoring for themselves. The business world of today is full of these examples where a manager will hire someone with a certain skill set to meet the need of the company. In return for the skill set the individual will meet the requirements set forth by the company. It is interesting to hear phrases like "Charlie is the life's blood of the company" and yet Charlie will find himself on the street when the company no longer has need of his particular set of skills. Corporations are designed to use the energies of those they employ as quickly as possible to ensure they get the most out of their investment. This is the result of 60 to 80 hour work weeks with no promise of a retirement or pension. Consider that many of those feeding on the successes of each other are working just as hard for the company to see profits only enjoyed by the few. The rest are diagnosed with anxiety, sleep, eating, or some other disorder....Of course it is the dis-order which is created by these institutions and many of these covens that run our worlds business today. In many ways a corporation is a breeding ground for some of the best apex predators on earth today. They know how to drain the energy and resources from those around them with a quick word and a smile without much effort or even appearing to do so. This is not limited to business, either. The family paradigm allows for the same type of feeding to occur. Families are setup to guide and raise children to become connected to themselves, but instead they are put on a field as soon as they know how to run and they are taught how to compete with each other. Soon the child is feeding off of the praises of their parents and they want more.

The vampires are great at manipulating people, but at first it may not be easy for you to pick out some of the vampires, while others are very obvious. With observation and time you will feel like you are the only one in the world who is witnessing the mass feeding frenzy. When people start labeling individuals as vampires, most will look for traits related to positions of power or those with status, but be careful it may be that this person is simply a zombie and following the rules of the company without giving it any thought. An easier mistake is labeling a person on the verge of being awake. Like you. You were a vampire as a child as a part of the energetic growth you experienced with your parents or significant mentors and guides. Do you believe you do not drain people today? Be careful with your

18

labels or desire to classify others until you can acknowledge your innate participation in these groups at different times in your own life. If you can do that today. Congratulations! That is evolution.

The best place to start recognizing the activities of vampires is to consider those closest to you. If you have family members who make you extremely tired if you are around them for any length of time it is because they are feeding on you and your energy. They will find a way to engage you in conversation about something that you are passionate about and they know the buttons that need to be pushed in order for you to put out the energy they seek. This effort is not unlike that of a four year old, which still feeds off the parents love and needs their attention all the time. If someone comes between them and their parent they are quick to require "attention". Look at the adult who is engaging you the same way and realize they never grew out of that phase. If you get emotional about this, you will be feeding them that energy. If you learn to remain neutral they soon move on to find another energy source. Vampires never identified the vast power which lies dormant within them and have not figured out how to connect to their own energy source, so they are feeding off of you.

Consider coworkers who will encourage you and get you fired up about a specific topic. They will get you so worked up that you feel that you need to do something about it. My favorite saying from a vampire is "I'm just saying", are perfect for defining the "Actions" of a vampire. With the vampire it is important to listen to words, but more important to watch their actions. Be aware the words of the vampire can be inspiring, even moving, but in many cases their actions do not match their words in any way, because "They are just saying". And that is all they do, is say. This is a telltale sign of identifying a vampire.

In the case of the zombie, their words match their action because the action is predictable. So when the vampire gets you to the point of action, where you are ready to do something about an event, turn around and ask the person if they are coming with you to address that issue. Since both of you are so fired up you should approach it together. The words "I'm just saying." will present themselves in some way. If the response to this is one of hesitation then you will know you have been fed on. Vampires are smart enough to feed off of a person's energy whether that energy is positive or negative. Understand that it is easy for the vampire to use any form of energy,

19

so they do not need to be directly involved with any issue you face. Now strategically the vampire knows in many cases it is better to let you confront an issue alone. This way it is a win-win situation for the vampire, if you lose your battle they will be there to console you and feed off of that energy, however, if you win they will be there to congratulate you and feed off of your energy. Either way the vampire is an apex predator and knows how to win the battle for energy... I'm just saying....

At first this may seem a little harsh because I am defining all young children as a vampire who feed off of their parents in the early years of their lives. The difference between an adult and a child is simple. The child is not aware they are pulling energy from their parents, they are learning. The energy they initially seek is based in love. As the child grows this sharing will change, but the hunger in the child grows. This is about the time a child starts attending school and playing with neighborhood friends. Want to guess what happens next? The child is feeding on the parent as much as the parent is willing to give the child, but the child now has other sources. The education begins. How did you find your way through this time in your life? How do you feed today? Still to soon? Okay let's keep going.

Today many parents are not aware that this is happening to them either, so it is hard for the parent to know how to teach the child about connecting to their source energy if they themselves do not understand the connection being created between them and their child. In some cases this may lead to the frustration of the parents and the potential isolation of the child. As a parent there are days when you see your child coming in the form of wanting your attention or excited about something they did during the day and you turned to them and say, "I am in the middle of something" or "give me just a minute." These are a parent's defense mechanisms to give themself a chance and prepare their energy for the invasion coming from the child. At the end of the day, when a mother looks so tired and pours herself into bed it may have nothing to do with the physical activities of the day and everything to do with how much energy their child required from them during the day. By the same token, when the child falls asleep at the dinner table it is obvious they have given just as much energy to the relationship. This will be discussed more in the following chapters, so we will focus here on those who should know better. Time for a test. Pay

20

close attention to your emotions when reading the following:
In my seeking to become more evolved or "aware", I have run across several books which really got me worked up. Many of them were just flat out wrong and taking advantage of people's naïve nature. This activity caused me to start writing a novel to the author to explain to them how wrong they were to infect others with their own version of reality and how their perspective was singular in nature as no one else had lived the facts of their life. Fortunately, I never sent any of these letters. Allow me a moment to respond to all those who would seek me out and wish to share their opinions with me about how wrong I am. My response to you might read something exactly like this.

Dearest   ,

I truly appreciate your thoughts and perspective when reading my book. It is easy to tell that you have great passion around your thoughts and beliefs as you expressed them in your recent comments to me. I am truly honored that you took the time first, to read my book, and then more importantly the time out of your busy day you took to write your perspectives down on paper or to talk to me in person about them. Please know I was able to be made more aware by your perspective and passion. I will take each of your points into consideration as I continue on my own path through this life and truly appreciate your inspiration. I am glad this book was as thought provoking for you as your comments have been to me. I wish you all the best in your future.

Respectfully yours,

Test complete. Did my words stir any emotion? Think about it before moving on.
Here is a vampires' trick when using energy. I set you up for an emotional experience. In the last paragraph I instigated a negative emotion simply by typing the word "wrong". The word spurs the ego to label a situation and believe there must be some rebuttal to being "wrong". You may have contributed to my words by defending my intended response. I had a negative impact on you based on my words. Then I pulled you in further by tying it to my response to a

21

person who took offense to my use of a word or perspective. If you have agreed with some of my words up until now you may have been ready to defend my letter to the would be aggressor. How did you feel in that space in that moment? Were you the offended person who does not agree with the words in my book? Did you put yourself "In their shoes" and attempt to be understanding? You may feel tricked by what I am about to say and my trickery is not as important as the moment you can have from it, so again put emotions aside before reading on.... Ready?

Now twist your perspective for a moment and imagine this response letter was to a fan of this book who absolutely loved it. They gave me rave reviews on-line and travelled hours for a book signing. Read the letter again with this new emotion. Does this letter read the same way? Imagine at a book signing I would turn to this specific page and sign my name to the signature line for this fan. The words are the same, but what has changed? Your label, your energy, your perspective?

I put a small bit of emotion and energy behind the negative label as part of the test, did you find yourself feeding it? If I invest just a little bit of energy and you invest more, than I can feed on that emotion and it is our emotion that often carries us down a path of sharing our energy with others.....In this example I chose to assign the words ahead of the letter to give you an emotional crutch for what you might experience. Then I showed you that you had been tricked to see a different perspective. In the end and without any emotion you realized that this same letter could be used by either a fan or a foe. It comes down to the emotion assigned to it. Often that emotion is provided by others and is what they rely on for their truth, either way. As a vampire I gave you your perspective, then showed you my response letter. You assigned emotions based on information I fed to you, then based on your perspective you put your own energy into it. This is why my focus in this book is on the questions, I feel, may be the most relevant based on my own journey. For me to provide you labels or answers would simply be those found in the reality I experience. Anyone who tells you they know how to show you the path to your personal awareness and growth better know everything about you or they are not being honest with you...or themselves.

I just explained to you how you feed off of others as a vampire and how vampires feed off of you, but this is my experience. Your perspective and emotions feed both zombies and vampires around you long enough for them to get involved and start feeding you. Yes, we chose to tie an emotion to the words in this book, where previously there was no emotion. You, the reader, instigated this emotion based on words I put on the paper, but ultimately must be the defining moments of your reality and can only be based on a perspective of the life you have lived….not I. The ability for man to tie to things in this manner make us brilliant and awake, full of potential and insight. Or it can make us energy sucking vampires and emotionally reactive zombies….. An excellent example of this is an amazing piece done by Jonathan Reed titled " I am part of a lost generation". If you Google this piece and allow it to play all the way through I am sure you will agree that perspective and emotions are powerful, sometimes blinding things.

Originally, this book was designed with techniques to help you live among the vampires and zombies. It has morphed into a book designed to further expand your state of self-awareness and will allow you the option to seek out your own questions while on your journey. I appreciate you sticking with me this long. If you agree with the information shared so far, give me time… I will get you uncomfortable somewhere along our journey together. If you are already irritated, we are going to have a wild ride!

23

IN THE BEGINNING…THERE WAS A BANG!

There once was a scientist, who was brilliant when it came to genetic coding and creating new species. The scientist decided to create a species which would include the coding for the existence of the scientists own brilliance. This was a way to guarantee the scientists work would continue through the species for all time. It would also ensure that the day would come when he would not be the only creator of living things. Many of us know this scientist by many different names. Names based on cultures and societies going back thousands of years. This scientist is the Alpha and the Omega, the source of all energy; the names given to the scientist through theologies are as numerous as the religions themselves. Then there are those who give the source no name at all because how do you apply language to something without comprehension or form? So for the purposes of this book we will settle on "the source" as being "God". To my knowledge there has been no one single, unilateral, cross culture, cross theological word that has EVER been agreed on by all of humanity…..So rather than starting a war about it, because we have been doing this for centuries, I will use the word God or scientist to describe that part of ourselves that is beyond our comprehension, but is a part of us all. The scientist found it critical to devise a superior species to all its' other creations. The scientist wanted to ensure they were given all the "bells and whistles", to this species, but found several challenges in doing this. Close your eyes and imagine being this form that is all that ever was and ever will be trying to create a form to represent a superior species…..This energy, you are imagining being, would have challenged itself to understand things from a place where it did not exist, because the concept of "being" or "ending" were abstract. Do you see this, could you imagine this? You should be able to, you are a part of it, now. Try this, think about your breathing…..Now when you are not thinking about it, it still happens, we understand we can control it, and why we do it, but do we remember a "beginning". This is the level of concept you must consider when you are thinking about the lack of there being a beginning for something that has always been, there is only abstract thought. Now, if you put yourself in that space and imagine the space with no understanding of the word beginning or end, then you will be closer

24

to understanding the space the scientist had in the lab. There was a limitation in the scientist by not being able to experience a beginning and no end. We do not remember our first breath and if you are reading this have yet to experience your last breath, but this is the concept we are talking about, so for all that is and ever was…this felt very limiting. Pondering this, the source energy gave birth to form and played with this form, according to Genesis, for six days. The source needed a place for this to occur, so like any good scientist created a lab with controls and laws to govern the conditions of the experiment. And according to Genesis this took the source five exhausting days to setup the lab. Now on the sixth day the Alpha and the Omega took on a great challenge by creating mankind. First, this form, of which the source has none, must be in the image and likeness of itself. So God has an ego? Why in the image and likeness of something without form? Unless this account was written by man…… That is the exploration of a different book.....The focus here is the creation of man, but raises an interesting question, since all of mankind bleeds and breathes the same way.

The challenge for God was to ensure the ability to participate in the experiment as an observer and experience the condition through observation, much like a parent living through the life of their child while screaming from the stands during a Saturday morning soccer game.

Below are how the scientist's notes might have been written.

Lab notes: Day 6- Creation of the scientist's Majestic Alternate Nature (MAN). In this blink I added a piece of self to this new form I am to call MAN. I gave it the gift of mortality so it could experience a beginning and an ending before returning to me. In this blink I spliced in a coding of my formless self to take on an image similar to what I could imagine myself to be, while retaining all the glory and magnificence of self. To create this MAN, I have created two versions of this new life form. I will use them to rule above all other forms created in the last five days. In the first blink of time, a portion of self must be crammed into each form to allow the experience to transfer back to the origin after a given period of time. This allows for the connection to be maintained and the form to be the entire source as it is now and has ever been. Further, I have created a slight difference in the form which will allow it to adapt to the location where it will exist. This has been a marvelous experiment resulting

25

in different sizes, shapes, and colors of this form. While the essential form will be consistent across all relative versions there will be variations as a result of the geographical locations. This was an unexpected variable discovered during the first blink, but I like it and it may bring about a wider variety of experiences for this form. Result: In this blink the form knew no difference from itself and source, except that it was confined to an existence of "weird" sensations. The MAN source did not like the separation and terminated the form returning to Source. There must be some other way to ensure the source form remains in that existence for a longer period of time.

Lab Notes…. Day 6, blink number two. I created a way to govern the form that would allow it to govern space and time. This is a magnificent form that is full of complexities and will allow the man form to use logic and reason while sustaining this form. This organ will be added to man so that man may apply reason and significance to its surroundings. I will call this version of man, 2.0 with a hardware upgrade of a brain.

Result: After attempting to add source to Man version 2.0 it was realized in half a blink that this logical being was able to reason away the need for suffering or experience of separation and returned to source… Version 2.0 was no more successful than the original version and additional work needs to be done.

Result: Blink number three. The complexity creation of this self-astounds me and it took less time to create concepts of light and dark as I head into my third version of man. I have determined that there needs to be yet another hardware upgrade to man in this version. This upgrade must include an organ that will tie the man to itself with the ability to tie itself to others of like form. For this reason I have decided rather than creating a single form of source that I will create two versions of source. From this blink forward I will use both forms of man and include all upgrades with both versions. This organ will be placed it the chest of both forms and will act as the bridge between the spark of self and the logical center placed in the head. My plan with this version is the desire and connection to self, created by the heart, will extend to the connection of others and will limit the desire to return to source.

Result: Yet again man version 3.0 was resistant to staying within the confines of the form created for source energy. This experience was able to last for a greater length of time and having the two

26

forms of self to connect to each other was a wonderful experience, however, this limitation of form quickly became a novelty that wore off and in less time than it took for the sun to move through an hour of darkness the human experiment terminated itself and returned to source.

Lab Log: At this point, I have created three versions of this form, each sustaining physical form longer than the last, however, each understanding its ability to return to source and having no ties to the human experience. So I have created a software upgrade for both forms in this version which I have called intellect. In this version I will limit the capacity of the brain to 50% utilization and allow both versions of this form to use this capacity to find self-importance and security based on one's own intellect.

Results: Man did not stay in form any longer than in the previous experiment, in fact the beauty of this brain, while taking it longer to process still came to the same conclusion and ended its physical condition very quickly. I am getting tired of this form ending its own existence and in the next software upgrade may right a rule that forbids this type of activity. It is important to limit the use and capacity of the brain in future versions. In fact one of the things which slowed this version down was a wonder and curiosity as to why they could only access 50% of their capacity. Still with that much access they unlocked the remaining potential very quickly and returned to source. In the coming versions brain capacity must become much more limited to ensure the human experience exceeds a single daylight hour.

Lab Log: Version five of this form will include software upgrades to the heart. While I continue to adjust the usable capacity of the brain I think the heart needs to act as the interface between the higher self and the brain. This will be the bridge and complete the trinity of man. With this organ wide open man is capable of sensing the higher self and accessing the brain in a way that allows it to open more of the brain for greater capacity and understanding. In order for the experience to continue for a longer period of time, I will incorporate emotions into the heart and a desire to survive, in form, to the brain. Emotions will cause the needs of the human experience to be driven by the need for safety and security, while seeking the love of others. In a way it is anticipated that the emotion software will also help in clouding complete access to the higher self except in the rare states of unconditional love.

27

Note: In next version set a variable that allows for attractions between these two versions towards, not only the self, but towards each other. These emotions will guide man on their experience, but will also cloud man's mind enough to keep them disinterested in returning to source so quickly. This sense of self will also bring about a drive for change in the experience, so the human condition will seek a variety of options and opportunities. This means I can create multiple copies from the templates, but the results can all vary depending on how I tweak the heart and mind of man. I am really excited about this version of man.

Result: Version 5.0 of man proved it was still a work in progress. While the feedback from these experiences has been wonderful, the experience itself is still too short. With the spark of origin remaining completely seen and an equal to the other upgrades it is only a matter of time before the spark desires to return to the source and the human form ceases to function. In the next version I will work on both timing and limitations of all three of these elements.

Lab Log: Version six is ready for testing. I have taken drastic measures with this version and determined that it is better to be too restrictive than allow for too much of any one element, so I have done the following: Brain capacity has been limited to approximately 8% utilization. This may make the human experience, "dumb as a stump", however, I have given them a set of software I call the Existence Guidance Order or EGO, to act as the drive and desires necessary to learn from mistakes and thrive in this world, while following the requirement to live with just that little of guidance. The heart too has been adjusted in both forms of man, emotional ties and responses have been increased to allow for a connection to self to be stronger and a drive or desire to tie to others. With the new versions I have included the ability to procreate and generate more versions of themselves allowing even stronger ties to the human experience and to the emotions that come with it. This solves the issue of the experience being too brief for any one part of self and allows time for the spark of origin to be manipulated by the other senses and organs before full maturity. As a matter of course, I want to ensure this spark is not permanently separated or unable to reconnect, so I have created blindness to the higher self at birth, I have also created an expiration date on physical forms that vary, but will end to each human experience, as to allow the spark to return to source.

28

Result: As this day draws to a close I have once again created something that may not last for very long. As man draws correlations with time and space I can only guess each human experience may only last several thousand years. This version of self is mentally handicapped to prolong the existence and has been filled with a variety of emotional responses to further cloud the spark of origin and prolong the human experience. At the same time, these elements may also cause this creation to destroy itself, ruin everything it touches, and consume each other and self before it is all said and done. In any case, it has taken me an entire day to create this version and when I activated it the conversation followed:

Man- Who are you?
God: I am your alternate nature.
Man: Who am I?
God: You are a Majestic Alternate Nature to all others.....You are MAN.
Man: Whoooa MAN......Who is that!?
God: Yes, that is woman.

Result: I have created a great version of self in man form and I have allowed that which was created to, itself, create. It has been given capacity to experience the great emotions of love, compassion, and connection, while at the same time being distracted by the minds logic to ensure the human form remains safe, has a "meaning" to exist for, and can do a variety of things to determine its' own fate. This all ties itself back to the higher self, which will scream in the background and try to be heard through the emotions and the logic of the heart and mind. The heart and mind will push the human experience forward for an evolution of the experiences. While creating this great trinity called man, I have realized it has also been given the capacity to destroy, to consume, and to manipulate their environments and be self-serving. These are an unexpected result of this experience and things I was not anticipating having the opportunity to experience, however, now I know that while, as a whole, I cannot experience these things, that I can experience them through my children in all their wonder and glory.

Results: There was an accident in the lab, kind of a big bang... For reasons I do not completely understand the energy in the lab took on its own momentum today and I became an observer as it all began to unfold. The creation, man, who was supposed to be the most magnificent creation of all and was supposed to oversee all

29

other creations got absorbed by the explosion and became a part of that creative process. The mix of heart, mind, and source energy was shuffled and the EGO software began running the MAN with some unexpected results. I have considered disassembling the lab and starting over, however, it has been magnificent to observe man and his struggles in the current state. To watch with intention as the MAN evolves himself and enjoy with wonder all those experiences I am not able to, as all that is, experience. I was intending on tweaking the heart and mind a little bit more so that evolution was easier for man, but have discovered that by having hidden the spark of origin from Man, it will extend his existence in this experience and as long as the higher self remains in denial, man will continue to have these experiences, until they have learned to broaden the mind and open the heart.....or they have destroyed themselves. This will be my last log entry because tomorrow, on the seventh day, my children have made me very tired... so I am taking tomorrow off! Note: I did make several modifications to the software for both the mind and heart. I found that this seems to be well accepted by the Man; where the heart is a bit more closed, and the mind is a bit more open and logic based. In the other version, the "wo-man" seems to thrive by having a more open heart and does not rely as much on the minds logic. While the software may be ideal in one model or the other I have decided that it may make sense to mix these software installs up occasionally to truly experience the brilliance of the human experience and allow man the opportunity to evolve and grow.   ---End of God Log for MAN---

30

As irreverent as this may sound to your own truth, it could have happened this way. Or any of the more than 2700 other theological belief systems which exist today and have been recognized as formal groups of likeminded hordes. Funny thing is, we are part of source energy, we were all there. We just need to re-member. If theologies never sat right with you in your heart have you asked yourself, why? Or are you still going and sharing your energy with other likeminded members of that social club?

One of my favorite jokes related to mans' creation is this:

God created the mule, and told him, "You are mule. You will work constantly from dusk to dawn, carrying heavy loads on your back. You will eat grass and lack intelligence. You will live for 50 years." The mule answered, "To live like this for 50 years is too much. Please, give me no more than 20." And it was so. Then God created the dog, and told him, "You are dog. You will hold vigilance over the dwellings of Man, to whom you will be his greatest companion. You will eat his table scraps and live for 25 years." The dog responded, "Lord, to live 25 years as a dog like that is too much. Please, no more than 10 years." And it was so.

God then created the monkey, and told him, "You are monkey. You shall swing from tree to tree, acting like an idiot. You will be funny, and you shall live for 20 years." The monkey responded, "Lord, to live 20 years as the clown of the world is too much. Please, Lord, give me no more than 10 years." And it was so.

Finally, God created Man and told him, "You are Man, the only

31

rational Being that walks the earth. You will use your intelligence to have mastery over the creatures of the world. You will dominate the earth and live for 20 years." The man responded, "Lord, to be Man for only 20 years is too little. Please, Lord; give me the 30 years the mule refused, the 15 years the dog refused, and the 10 years the monkey rejected." And so God made Man to live 20 years as a man, then marry and live 30 years like a mule working and carrying heavy loads on his back. Then, he is to have children and live 15 years as a dog, guarding his house and eating the leftovers after they empty the pantry; then, in his old age, to live 10 years as a monkey, acting like an idiot to amuse his grandchildren.

Perspective is an interesting thing.

THE ETERNAL CHILD

If our life was truly designed to have a fate, then as a parent wouldn't we design the fate of our offspring as our scientist has done for all his children? Or do we truly want our children to design a fate that is the life they desire to live? Be careful here, a parent "scientist" will have no less love and desire for his offspring then we do for ours. After all we were made in the image and likeness of..... The answer depends on how much we allow our ego to stand in our way. But the source is not limited by ego, so wouldn't any parent or that of any God want their offspring to follow their desires? It would be in service to our parents for us to pursue our bliss, and in service of our higher power to use our will to experience our life to its' fullest potential; by determining those trials which will help us create our fate, not by having one dictated to us. Enter the Eternal child who lives within all of us and was the greatest gift from the scientist. Unfortunately, not all of us have recognized the gift exists or we have recognized it and chosen to ignore it.

By listening to this child we can determine our bliss. Through bliss we determine a path which makes us happy. Unfortunately, today our children learn at some point that what makes them happy is not what society wants from them and so the child is told to "put away childish things" and stop listening to that inner voice. This is the beginning of our disconnect and is when we become powerless to hear our own desires.

Loa Tzu, a Chinese philosopher over 2500 years ago stated, "the biggest problem with the world is that individuals experience themselves as powerless." A child may feel dependent or helpless in the first years of their lives. These are not powerless individuals, they are helpless, but also full of love and the grace from the source making them all powerful. If a child's youngest years are spent being abused and made to feel fear then they may learn to feel helpless and the illusion of being powerless, but none of us are ever less than magnificent. It does not matter what others say about us, we are a part of source and a part of those with a desire to repress that power. So while our physical form may be helpless, our spirit, is never powerless. As an adult we may feel, at times, trapped or helpless and this may lead to experience fear. This is what it means to believe you are enslaved by circumstances you may perceive as being beyond your control, or "your fate".

This is how we perpetuate the next generation into becoming

33

zombies and the eternal child will be repressed within the person, unable to be heard through the fear and noise. It will remain this way until there is a life-changing event. This can be as simple as a random act of kindness or as dramatic as a near death experience. For me it was a poem by Marianne Williamson titled "Our Greatest Fear".

Our Greatest Fear

Our deepest fear is not that we are inadequate.
Our deepest fear is that we are powerful beyond measure.
It is our light not our darkness that most frightens us.
We ask ourselves, who am I to be brilliant, gorgeous,
talented and fabulous?
Actually, who are you not to be?
You are a child of God.
Your playing small does not serve the world.
There's nothing enlightened about shrinking so that other
people won't feel insecure around you.
We were born to make manifest the glory of
God that is within us.
It's not just in some of us; it's in everyone.
And as we let our own light shine,
we unconsciously give other people
permission to do the same.
As we are liberated from our own fear,
Our presence automatically liberates others.
—Marianne Williamson

Twenty five hundred years after Loa Tzu wrote those words, feeling powerless is still the root of tragedy within humanity. In our heart, we know how spectacular we really are, but because of our mind and the manipulation of others we have hidden it. It is ironic that our brilliance hides like a fearful child in the dark when we could be cooperating with each other as powerful members of humanity in harmony with the world around us, as if a child on the playground. I know it sounds idealistic to have everyone following their bliss, but it is not. We will always struggle to show our true selves because our true nature is scary. It is the brightest light and the darkest shadow. It is heart and ego. In this genuine nature of self we all have the

34

opportunity to see society for what it is and ask the question "Why?" The resulting work from this question from everyone, at once…Less than ideal and far from Utopian. What I am saying is not idealistic, it is generations of hard work. Ready?

What happens when people see you living your dream? When you reach out to excel or want to initiate change? The first thing many people will say to you is "Be careful" or " make sure you are not risking it all," these are the zombies. Then there are those who encourage you to go and conquer the world, without any personal commitment, then wait for you to succeed or fail to feed off of it. Like a vampire. When you have attained your bliss, then these same people will become frustrated with themselves and find a way to make it your issue or will "hitch a wagon" to you and go along for the ride ......

As I mentioned earlier, in the playground example, the eternal child in all of us has taken a beating over the last several decades. It is not hard to see why people need to have a mid-life crisis or need to spend three hours a week with a therapist. It is the cry of the eternal child within all of us trying desperately to remind us that we are powerful and that we must remember to find our passion, to follow our bliss. Unfortunately, in society today if you are on the playground and you have not brought a child you may see parents scoop up their children and leave the area. Worse yet you may be having a conversation with a police officer about what it is you're "really doing" at the park by yourself just watching the children play, this is sad. Not as sad as watching the brilliance in children who play together without a second thought of skin color or manner of clothing. Sad knowing that all that will change for them as they get taught they are not brilliant, that they do not know, and that they are powerless to change any of it.

While dating in my early 20's my girlfriend and I double dated with some of her friends and went to a playground at 11:30pm in a local neighborhood. We sat on the swings and talked. We were not drunk, we were quiet and respectful of the darkened homes around us, we were just having a good time. I felt very uncomfortable because I was not a kid anymore and why would the others want to come to a playground? Then a part of me, that eternal child, asked why I was not willing to have fun anymore? Where did I lose the desire to have fun? When did you lose it? Why did I put away my eternal childhood things? The short answer, it was what society

35

expected of me and I did not want to disappoint. Sure it is an easy answer now, but it took years of life experiences and hours of introspection to come up with the answer I asked myself on the playground that evening.

Approximately a year later, I was introduced to the writings of Joseph Campbell when I was in college, this happened by "accident". I was looking for an easy class to fill my English requirements and one of my options was a class titled The Powers of Mythology. The class description made it seem as though the class centered on Greek and Roman mythical gods. Since this was an area I always enjoyed I signed up for the class. One of the books that was required reading in this class was a book by Joseph Campbell titled "The Power of Myth" and I soon realized that I would not be learning about Greek or Roman gods, but instead learning about similarities between theologies. I found myself getting off the bus one day saying to myself "There is a God, there is a God!!" This class got me very frustrated, but also very interested in the concepts of myth and since I spent 12 years in catholic schools I was able to bring a certain level of understanding to the conversation. While I cannot recite or remember much of what he said in his book I can remember my reaction to one quote. Before his passing he encouraged people to "follow your bliss", and I remember thinking "Yeah right, I have student loans, classes, work, and other obligations. I do not have time to follow my bliss." The reason this quote stuck out was not because of the profound nature of it, but my negative response to it. I had several of these moments in this class and this made it one of the best classes I ever took during my college education or graduate work.

If I had to point back to one moment in time when I began waking up and really wanting to stay awake it was following my response to this quote. I was shocked that I would respond in such a way when somebody was just telling me I needed to be happy in my life and I was saying "What right do I have to do that!" I followed this up with "Why don't I do this?" The answer I came to was expectations. My expectations of self based on my culture and society. The society was not built to ensure bliss and I was starting to understand that I had been asleep.

I gave this more thought when I discovered that Joseph Campbell collaborated with George Lucas to create an epic story of a boy's quest for manhood and search for his father. Mr. Lucas created a

36

classic using an age old story and told it using technology to support the framework of the story. He created the movie "Star Wars". It was at this point in my life in that class that I realized I would never grow to understand anything new if I only read books of people who viewed the world the same way I did. The real growth, for me, came from reading books I disagreed with and listening to the perceptions of people where I shared no common ground. Is this possible for you to do in your life? Years later, I came to see there is no such thing as conversing with a person with no common ground. Do you know why? Of course you know why!! You are the same magnificent energy at the core of your being. We are all energy and at the end of this life we are all going to transform into an alternate state of that energy. This we all have in common, you just need to reconnect...to re-member with your SELF which you have hidden away.

The truly amazing thing was that I had followed in the footsteps of many of those who came before me who seemed happy and I believed that if I waited long enough, worked hard enough, put in my time, then I too would be happy. In actuality, I realized that I was in Rome and pretending to be a Roman, so I would fit in and not be fed to the lions. And so the saying goes "When in Rome you do as the Romans do", so I was living in that world and euthanized my inner child to find the happiness I was supposed to have by following the ways of others, but instead of using my powerful nature for the important work, I learned how to fake it and still have fun with my family and friends, the zombies!

Want to have some fun as an observer? When you go to the airport take a walk up and down the concourse and play this game I call "guess where". The object of this game is to guess where people at a certain gate are going before looking at the kiosk. Since you have an hour before your flight it is not hard to find time to play this game and get in a little exercise. As you walk down the concourse look at the people waiting for the plane to board, are they smiling and having fun? Are they wearing suits or are they dressed tropical? Then once you have guessed "fun" or "dud" look at the airplane destination. If you do this often you will be able to figure out if the plane is headed to Cancun or California before you look at the kiosk, then who on the flight is excited about the flight and who is dreading the flight. Soon you will be able to tell who is on their honeymoon, or who is anxious about flying simply by observing their

37

actions.

One word of caution when playing this game, don't stare.....Again another trait vampires look for is someone who is having inspired or conscious thought. Their reaction is usually aggressive and overbearing, this allows them to take your energy from you and feel justified in doing it. You feel embarrassed for staring and they feel invigorated from being aggressive. Leave the sleeping zombie and aggressive vampires lie....at this point.

Let's use another movie as an example of the eternal child. In the movie "The Matrix" Neo, played by Keanu Reeves was receiving mentoring and instruction in a martial arts dojo. This scene was very entertaining and filled with special effects, however, the words shared between Neo and his instructor was priceless. In essence Neo had been asleep and his instructor was trying to awaken him so that he would understand his full potential. We see the struggle every day in our own lives and while it does not take place in a dojo or have the latest special effects; the sparring occurs between ourselves and our eternal child every day. The beautiful thing is I see the eternal child winning in more situations today than ever before. This is the struggle we must first win with the humanity within ourselves and then we will see the change in our societies. There is a saying "Man plans and God laugh's". This saying is one of my favorites because it puts into perspective for me that while we are making all of these plans for ourselves, our inner child is also the one laughing at us during this human experience. So from that perspective, yes I plan every day and there is indeed a part of me laughing at myself, daily. Wait, back up.....Did I just refer to myself as God? Peddle harder now you are getting to the crest of that hill......

Ask yourself, doesn't theology root itself in the concept of there being a part of ourselves that is greater than the human experience can comprehend? As parents we provide the genetic makeup of our offspring. This genetic makeup provides our offspring with traits similar to our own and we know that a part of us will live in them, but a child will cease to exist if that child is only fed physically. It is the other part of self that must be fed and energized through love for the physical form to flourish. In this case, I am the father of my child. So it would stand to reason that the source created all humanity making humanity the child of the source. Regardless of how you wish to define the source or the theology you choose to follow there is

always a connection between the source and its offspring that is not physical. This must also mean that each of us are connected to each other through this same energy. We are siblings making us a part of each other and all a member of the source…..Now where do you feel the source must reside? In you? In me? In all things?
 Ahh, siblings and what do all siblings do when they are young? They fight with each other and they all vie for their parent's time, attention, and approval. Has it become obvious yet? Are you seeing a pattern where the eternal child of humanity was separated from source to be able to experience things in a separate, yet connected "human form"? By doing this the human form created greater separation from self and others as a child would do from a sibling. Isn't it interesting that through this experience we can still be a child, by using this experience to further separate ourselves. Is it any wonder that there are those in the world today who feel completely alone and separate? Doesn't it amaze you that we can be so technologically advanced and yet still not see the core which is central to us all?
If you have ever had the opportunity to be in a maternity ward or have held a newborn child you have come very close to your eternal child. With any newborn I have noticed that when I hold them they all smell the same….The nursery in a maternity ward smells the same. I like to think that this is the smell of the higher self. The infinite, limitless part of us all crammed into this tiny form and is still oozing from every pore of the newborn. That essence is pure love and limitless energy and we can feel it pulsating through us as we hold that child. If I were to go back to my religious roots I may be inclined to say, "filled with the Holy Spirit", but how can I be any of this if I myself, even while in the form, did not maintain that spark of origin? How could any of us? When I return to source of all love, I will not be separate, but a part of the source bringing with me all my human experiences. I just hope the download process is not similar to the spike they shove in the back of Neo's head in the movie The Matrix.
Theoretically, this might mean that this spark…..this soul…..Can only be source energy or…..God. I can accept that this is separate from me or consider it is that part of me that is my eternal child. Along for the ride through our human experience and only takes control when our physical experience has ended. I have the same question for you ….How can you not believe that your higher self is

39

an element of the source, the God or whatever you desire to name that which is greater than yourself and yet is the greatest part of you? Maybe you have never had the opportunity to experience it? Maybe admitting it is there would mean you would also have to accept that it also exists in every other human being on the planet? In your mind there is a yelling and screaming battle raging. This battle lives in your logic center and echoes what it knows you have been taught about these things. It echoes what you have been taught is the truth, but take a moment and try to hear what is going on in your heart? Is it possible that your heart is emanating a whisper and trying to tell you that we are the best part of the creator as our children are the best part of us?

I think this is a good place to discuss the difference between being awake and being enlightened because at first glance the two may seem to be the same. I will ask you to read with your heart and try to see the trap in this next section before I announce it to you. As you read the following words your mind will take you down a path, but the exercise is designed to enable you to hear your heart. It is a trap for your brain. You have been warned, so here goes.

To be awake simply means the ability to see people and situations for what they are with the ability to balance your responses while participating in the world according to the reality of others. A person who is awake finds comfort in being able to easily slip back into zombie mode when things get tough or draw energy from others when they are tired. This is where I prefer to live because to be enlightened is a whole different level. To be enlightened simply means you have accepted how powerful you are and how instrumental you can be by assisting other people to find their bliss and acknowledge their eternal child, in a very active way. To slip back into being a zombie or vampire is a waste of time and energy. They can quite there mind without meditation and can live in their own reality while the reality of others swirls around them.

So which is better? Are you still wrapped up in your mind trying to figure out where you fit in and what is your label? Have you figured out that having a physical life is a lot of work? The work we do is no different than the struggles others have conquered. You are not awake, enlightened, a Bob or Frank or Susan. You are not a label, so do not allow yourself to be walked into a situation where someone, like me, offers to tell you how they self-identify and then define you through a label. It is a trap used every day by vampires.

40

It is too simple a label for any being as impressive as you. My preferred label, the village idiot, allows me to walk through this world without worrying about how to improve my label.

Being awake still allows you the luxury of being passive with the world, being enlightened means you are active with everything around you. In the end, again, it is all about how you grow your own awareness as a part of a much larger whole. I am talking universal, not species. Stop limiting your self to the temporary nature of this species. Your impact on it will be fleeting, but what you can learn about yourself while you are in the experience, that is priceless.

In the movie "With Honors" a young man was preparing to graduate from college at the top of his class and he had everything going for him. He was focused, motivated, and dedicated to his society's cause. He was a great zombie and very passive in his life. Unfortunately, early in this movie he ran into an "enlightened" bum played by Joe Pesci. During the course of this movie you saw this young man "wake up", but saw the frustrating internal struggle of him as he became active in his own life. The movie did a good job showing some of the challenges he faced by being awake. In the final 15 minutes of the movie it was evident that this character had become enlightened. In this case he knew the consequences of his actions may have negative impacts on his future, however, his fate was something he determined based on listening and following his eternal child. So being awake does not require that you take action, instead when enlightened the opportunity to take action is presented and executed by the person even though they are fully aware of the results and the fate they have created for themselves.

Keep in mind vampires are awakened often by the eternal child. The more often they are awakened the clearer their actions become to them. Often they will seek out inspiration, but may not like the work they find. During these times it is important to realize that they do not always take energy from someone with the goal to drain that person. In fact, there are times that the vampire will give energy, love, and support to ensure that you interact with them at a later time. A motivating boss who inspires you to finish a project, only to discover later that they took credit for your work. Vampire. They inspire so that they may feed off you later on when you confront them or silently seethe about their actions. Either way they can feed off this energy and still take credit for your accomplishments.

This may seem depressing at first, but consider that a vampire who

41

is awake is trying desperately to find a source of energy, love, or even hate that will quench their thirst. The eternal child in them presents them with opportunities to seek out and find a way to connect back to the source, but they cannot see or hear it because their mind is screaming at them about the labels and power required to be a successful person. In turn they may learn to become an even better vampire.

I would hope we all come into this world with the ability to feed on all the love the world has to offer. We all start as vampires with the opportunities to evolve, standstill, or slide into a state of being numb. As we grow, we become stronger in our ability to connect to others and draw energy from them. The hope is that we have been mentored by our parents, guides, or major influences and shown how to connect back to source to maintain our own energy levels without needing to draw the emotional energies from others before ourselves. Before ourselves? What does this mean? It is a heart question. Where are you able to draw the greatest amount of energy? From someone else? Or from yourself?

Imagine a friend who is all about the drama. They talk louder than they need to, are more expressive with their body movements and exert a lot of energy. Where do they get all of that energy? Are you feeding them? If not, then are they feeding you? If they were not so dramatic about things would they still be a friend? Easy to answer all of these questions with your head, but I am not challenging you to use that organ to answer these questions.

Unfortunately, many times these types of questions are too difficult or the answers seem to elusive for those seeking change. So instead we live in the logic of our head, but this is not where the energy of love is created and as a result there is often a twisted form of love manifested as a result. This form of love can be the result of frustrations, peer pressure, or other life events causing us to just want to go back to sleep or worse yet to give up and walk through the world in the sleep state of a zombie.

It is in this struggle that many of us have found ourselves, today, trying desperately to listen to the eternal child. The struggles that we have with our society and the root problems that we have with the evolving of humanity are centered in the choices that we make today. The decisions to be asleep or awake are only the first steps. Consider the popular bumper sticker I have seen on vehicles with the word "coexist", while in theory this seems like a great step

42

forward it is really a step nowhere. The bumper sticker should read "evolve already" this means we are ready to step forward away from the concept of needing to find a way to "coexist". Our humanity should be beyond this struggle needing to find a way or reason to coexist. Instead, when we do evolve there will be no reason to require people to find a way to coexist. And the concept of needing to coexist already seems laughable to the eternal child within each of us.

In every great vampire story or movie it is the vampire that misses their humanity or some part of it. In many cases the movies and fiction are designed around the concept of a vampires need for evolution or love. Either wanting to be something they are not or to be loved for who they are. At the center of this struggle is usually a woman. Is your mind screaming at you because of my gender bias? If it is silence it and stick with me so you do not miss my points.

It is usually a woman who reminds the vampire of this loss of self or love and so a great story is told around that journey. This is not just a great story; it is a reality for you today. Some of you are those vampires in the business world today who are feeding off of the ingenuity and independent thought being created by the zombies. Some of you are living a day to day existence occasionally waking up when interrupted by a defining moment and there are those of you on the cusp of being in touch with your eternal child.

Regardless, all of us are on a journey. One being no more important or more enlightened than the next. In each of these cases some sort of crisis can be expected.

Crisis occurs for the vampire when they wake up to the fact that what they are doing is in direct opposition of their heart and their own eternal child. Consequences related to coming to this reality can be….violent. This is one reason I strongly encourage you at several places in this book to take these exercises and questions slow. Be very gentle with yourself and your discoveries. Remember that a lifetime of experiences taught you how to be the person you are today, so changing that for something different will take time. Be patient with yourself and with those around you. Remember those around you are associating with you because of the person you have always been, when you change that it is likely that your relationships will change, also. So take it slow and be kind.

IF YOU CAN'T BEAT THEM.....TRY HARDER

Step one and the easiest step for most of us is to continue with the status quo. There are a lot of people in this world who are trying desperately to wake up, but are struggling and cannot find the support they need to move out of a place where they feel powerless. Not only that, but they are surrounded by noise. A lot of noise. Everyone with Internet access and an e-mail account is aware of junk mail. This is unsolicited electronic mail that you did not ask for and do not want, but find yourself having to deal with it from time to time. Junk mail is a type of noise. It distracts you from what is really important and if you are not careful the junk mail can steal your identity. Life has a lot of junk mail and many of us can't help looking at it and even listening to some of the useless noise it produces in our brains.

Many of us have been trained or taught that we have to look at it and listen, if for no other reason to make sure we are not missing anything important. In life we are overwhelmed with junk mail not all of it malicious, however, again perspective can be a tricky thing. I watched an interview with Barbra Streisand where she explained to a reporter that she was on stage one day and a person was holding up a sign that said, "I love you Barbara". Mrs. Streisand explained the profound effect that this had on her "perspective". She did not know this fan as a person and was now coping with a type of noise because this fan did not have any idea who Barbra Streisand was as an individual. While this was not malicious in intent and this fan adored her for her skills as a singer and actress, it was junk mail she had to learn how to deal with on an ego level.

I have a great deal of empathy for every child actor I have seen manipulated by the institutions of fame. To take a young child and put them in an environment where they have everything they could ever want, are told they are loved, and are sharing this experience with those around them only to find out that many of those around them are vampires and zombies. When the child wakes up they

44

have a very inflated ego and perception of self. When they come to see the manipulation by those who "loved" them, they are lost. They have no idea how to find that eternal child and have been taught nothing about how powerful they are, inside. What they know as power comes from money and title. They then become the manipulators, but because they have not been taught these skills either, many of them end up with very difficult lives. For us this creates a new world of junk mail many like to feed off of. There is even a whole industry built around getting the dirt on those who are famous and "exposing" them. Lest we forget they are still human. This is very similar to the movie Jim Carrey performed in 1998 called "The Truman Show". This movie walks you through the emotions a man experiences when he finds out his life has been constructed for him, but his life has never been about him, it was always about the ratings. While the movie was not one of Carey's best efforts it brought a point home about humanity and how fascinated we are with others' lives. Why do you think that is? Could it be more noise to keep us distracted from working on our own evolution?

Depending on the support system, when the ride is over a child actor may come face-to-face with the facts that it was all a big show and was never really about them, it was about the money and the ratings, what follows for that person at a very young age may resemble a life crisis if there is not a suitable support system in place for them. What they have been told about love, about the world they live in, and about themselves really did nothing to serve them, but instead served the people who wanted something from them. As the shine lost its luster on the child's career many of the self-serving vampires found "the next best thing" and abandon the child to deal with their own fallout. You have a favorite actor in your head that you saw this happen to. What do you feel for them now? Has your perspective changed or is that "Just the price of fame"? Does there have to be a price for following your bliss? Why do we feed this frenzy by paying paparazzi to hound these folks day and night? To make us feel better about our lives when we see that they spent the night in jail? NOISE! Yes, if you buy nationally publicized magazines to read the latest about your favorite star, you are funding these people and are feeding on your favorite stars latest success or misery. People enjoy reading and viewing these photos to show themselves that these people are human, also.

45

Unfortunately, for many child actors they were never told they were a human being, but that being human would take some time and training. Essentially, these people are saying I want to be fed on by zombies and vampires and open themselves up to this world in return for fame. Humanity will feed on these people in the days of their success and subject them to invasions of privacy in the name of fame. This means people believe it is okay, if a person is famous, they have no privacy. This is like saying that water has no business being wet. In the end, this industry is only supported because of the amount of energy the masses of zombies put into it. The junk mail in any human being's life can be overwhelming and demand a lot of attention, but for a child actor there is even more junk mail that must be sorted through, worked out, and in many cases deleted, so they need a good mentor, guide or parent to guide them through this lifestyle.

Consider for a moment if you wake up every morning to find that the person who said to you "your awesome, your great, and everybody loves you" has suddenly left you. This is not your spouse; this is your agent. The support you have had for five years is suddenly packing up their bags and leaving after telling you for so long how much they love you. This may feel much like a divorce, but in the case of an actor the entire support system is removed or changed. The actor does not understand the type of love that was being given came with many conditions and contracts. In many cases the actor, as a child, was never exposed to the concept of unconditional love; there had always been a trade of one thing for another. The child had never learned to love themselves, so now the ability to be courageous and bold with the new changes is something they cannot conceive getting past. It is during this time that these people need genuine caring individuals around them who can act as mentors and guides, otherwise, these children end up in court, on drugs, or dead because as a society we have not prepared them to be awake, but they do not want to be asleep. We have set them up with fame, put them on the covers of magazines, held up posters telling them how great they are, and sent them fan mail. For the actor, in many cases, this is all junk mail that cannot be ignored and much of it often dictates the type of person they need to be for their fans, regardless of who they want to be. In the public eye, there is an expectation for them to act a certain way and so they have learned to be a part of the crowd and what the crowd wants them to

46

be. Can you contemplate the collision course this person is on? There are excellent actors, who have navigated this world, have had the opportunity to really find themselves and appreciate who they are; while following their bliss, but this is the minority of actors, especially children actors. It would be nice to see the actors take on a mentoring program where they work with children coming into the limelight who will be challenged with all the fame and all the energy, but who are not sure how to balance it all. This is the concept of paying it forward which is something we will discuss in a later chapter.

Now let's look at the business world, to keep your job and get promoted you must imitate the styles and actions of the zombie or vampire. While we discussed that the zombie uses a group mentality to consume the energy and physical traits of those around them. We also know the overall experience and energy becomes absorbed then used by the group. Those people who try desperately to stay awake throughout their lives find themselves constantly in a place where they are drained both mentally and physically by those around them. It is the group that is the addiction, so if you can become independent of the group then the personal energy will start to increase. Migraine headaches and physical sickness are common occurrences for people who are trying to understand their world and remain awake, but are also common for those trying to get out of the zombie daze. This can be extremely frustrating to anyone who is trying to stay awake, but find themselves being constantly pulled or choosing to walk back into the group. The advice for the zombies, again, is to take it slow. This is not a "cold turkey " process. It took years to get in the group and to get established. Now you want to change gears. Start by taking a walk by yourself, listen to the sound of your footsteps and your breathing for 30 minutes. Your goal, to quiet your mind, to reduce the noise level of the day. Then with time start observing the activities of your group without taking from it. Begin listening to what the voice inside you starts to say, more importantly listen for the whispers.

The workplace also includes those who would be considered a vampire class co-worker. This coworker is more evolved than the zombie and where the zombie does not like to pursue management roles, these co-workers are on "the fast track". They are fast and they do not require others in order to consume energy or manipulate

47

the constraints of their environment. These are your co-workers who will do anything to get ahead and if they view you as a threat, they will create a plan for dealing with you, also. The coworker vampire is probably the most draining of all because they only see you as a place for them to feed. The interesting thing is that the co-worker vampire is probably the one class who take the most opportunities to become awake. The zombies and vampires are offered the same numbers of opportunities, but the vampires see these more often. Why do you think a vampire will pursue being awake more often than the zombies?

In either case the person trying to find their way out of this nightmare may find themselves giving up and becoming a member of either society. This is the first option and has to be mentioned because in our society today there is nothing wrong with "an honest day's work for an honest day's pay", if you can find that situation many people will give up their dreams to be able to be comfortable and sleep through their lives. The problem is, one day something may happen that will cause this person to wake up, will cause them to realize that what they have, is not really what they want. Many of us identify this as a "midlife crisis."

Through the course of this guide I have said our societies and cultures are imitated through Internet and television. Consider also that it is through the most inspirational books and television shows that we find ourselves waking up looking around and seeing just how many people are still consuming the human experience in some twisted form of love. Technology provides a bridge for inspiration, as well as the opportunity to be drawn into distraction and a much deeper sleep.

At this point in your experience, the safest thing, by far, is to remain asleep and be a zombie going to your 9-to-5 job, collecting your paycheck, watching mass media, falling in line with what you're told to do, and how you are supposed to act. So it is not hard to see why the first step that you can take in this guide is really to take no step at all and to just remain a part of the group. Well, this is an option, right? As the saying goes "If you can't beat them, join them" and if you believe it is hopeless then you can stop peddling at this point, put the book away, and go back to sleep.

In this theory of evolution, the lowest life form is that of the zombie. We all started off as a vampire, but as we discovered we can give up on humanity and slip into the zombie state of being. Dim our light

48

and turn away from the path allowing others to shine brightly while we blend into the crowd. These crowds rely on the institutions of the world to tell them how to act, what to wear, to buy, and how to perceive their world. They are in fact told everything they need to know from the time they wake up in the morning, until the time they go to sleep at night.

On occasions children have evolved into master vampires themselves, by imitating the actions of their parents, teachers, or friends. I believe that it is the vampire that inevitably evolves through the process of an awakening, but even the vampire has a difficult time understanding how to remain awake because of the social and cultural pressures. The easiest way to do this is to feed on the energy of those zombies around them while they continue to evolve and discover that they do not need to feed on others at all. Unfortunately, the vampires in this adolescent state must feed and it has an inexhaustible hunger. They have not figured out that the inexhaustible supply of energy they seek has always been within them. It is not external.

When my daughter was three years old she met her grandfather for the first time. As a three year old and by her own nature, she was extremely shy, even fearful of people she did not know. So it was extremely exciting to see my daughter approach her grandfather with her arms open wide, climb into his arms, and put her head down on his shoulder for a full two minutes without moving. This was a little girl who you could not get to stop moving from the time she rose in the morning to the time she collapsed in her bed at night. Here she was very quiet and very still resting in her grandfather's arms and absorbing energy very rapidly. The nice thing is he was very aware of what she was doing and had tied himself back to source energy and giving her energy on an unconditional basis of love. They still have a very strong connection to this day. This type of connection is what we all need. It is how zombies maintain their strength and what vampires crave from others. At some point we all receive it, unfortunately many do not understand what they have received or only understand later in life when they have been walking around in a daze for years or maybe even decades.

While much fewer in number the vampire maintains a greater level of self-awareness. If you have transitioned or never left this state, then it too is a safe place to be for you. The vampire has learned to have a certain level of power and charisma over situations. They can manipulate both people and circumstances to their greatest advantage. This usually involves feeding on those that work for them or with them then using that energy to better understand themselves. The vampire will feed quickly and move on, to avoid being challenged by the energy of an entire zombie horde. Again, if you are only going to follow step one in this process then joining the vampire coven and "creating the flow" is only just a step above being a part of the zombie mob where they "go with the flow". The vampires excel at creating "the flow". The challenge facing the vampire is their thirst is never quenched, so they use their charisma for dark purposes and drain others energy as they need it. The transition from vampire to being awake occurs when the person sees others for who they truly are, is willing to accept that, will do the right thing in spite of that, and is aware of the potential cost of them standing against an established society of zombies and institutions of vampires.

For a vampire trying to awaken it is possible that everything they have worked so hard to achieve within this society or institution may be lost. Being awake has many benefits, but also many drawbacks. The goal here is to focus on the benefits and minimize the drawbacks, but understand this may cost friends and even a way of life you have grown accustomed to having. On the upside, you will not miss them once you move into this space.

So it stands to reason that the most dangerous place to be is where many people find themselves today. When they have a "defining moment" which inspires them or causes them to wake up they get noticed by those around them. Those around them are anxious to feed off of the inspiration and energy being provided by the person who is woken up, but are not really driven by the inspired thought as much as by the energy it is creating. The force of a common energy in a single room can be overwhelmingly and loving. Can you think of a time when groups of people meet and generate loving energy? Vampires are drawn to these places and exist here in the hundreds. They will gather, feed and then cannot wait to get away from the others. Give up? In my experience there are massive amounts of energy generated when people gather for prayer or meditation. If your tired after church on Sunday, it may not have been because of the party you went to the night before.

There is also the possibility this energy can generate the opposite of

50

love in certain situations. One of these situations is sporting events. Think of a stadium full of people where a fire begins to consume the stadium. The energy in the stadium shifts. Can you feel it in yourself right now? Can you be in the stadium and sense the level of energy in others? If you were there you would; as one person panics, then another, and another. Soon everyone is panicking, running each other over and the entire horde is now driven by fear and the desire to survive. Energy reaches a person before the mind panics. The energy contributed by each individual will move like a shockwave to everyone around them during this time. Why? Why are we so interconnected at these moments of crisis? Are we just as connected during our moments of love? Would everyone in the stadium panic? Who is most likely going to panic? Fear is as powerful as love and fear is how you convince a nation of people that genocide is a good idea. In this scenario is has to do with the energy being fed to the masses in a state of fear, but is not different than the energy being piped into the church during Sunday mass. Can you determine what energy is being fed to the masses today? Is it Love? Fear? Who is generating it….And Why?

When your next defining moment happens, if not careful, with who and how you share it, you will get attention. Others will try to consume your energy in that moment, to be consumed by either the masses or fed on by a vampire.

Hitler did not almost take over the world on his own, he had masses of vampires and zombies ready to consume the world based on his ability to manipulate and manage fear. Sadly our current day challenges have not changed that much in terms of how people feed on energy or how mass media has prioritized what is fed on. The steps in this guide were designed to help those of you interested in peddling faster for that hill. You are now starting to ask the right questions and the inspiration of others will find you, if you are looking for it and willing to act on it when you see it. This inspiration will help you to navigate through the masses of zombies and cunning predators. If you are ready to continue you will find yourself in for one hell of a ride. The real question is this: Given that this world is full of vampires and zombies do you really want to wake up? Do you want to live in this reality? Or do you want to do what you did in kindergarten and put your head down on the desk for your nap and go back to sleep for the rest of your life as a member of society?

51

WHEN IN ROME....FAKE IT

ALRIGHT! So you have decided that step one is not for you and you want to be awake, however, you do not want to "rock the boat" with your family, your employer, or your life all at once. Here we will discuss how to remain awake while in your current situation's and pretend to be a part of the crowd while growing strong enough in your new reality. This will give you time to become more comfortable about remembering what you know. You will see things become clearer and scarier at the same time. When it is scary remind yourself you are on the right path because this is when you are most like a child. The difference is a young child has no idea that they should be afraid and an adult is oversensitive to it. You will need to find the middle ground while walking through this step. Children are great observers, naturally curious, fearless, and genuine. We can learn a lot from the child and how they view life as an observer. The art of being a conscious observer is the first step to being able to fake your way through life in the presence of zombies and vampires.

Consider these two phrases: "driving a car" and "riding a motorcycle". Why is it not phrased driving a motorcycle?

The difference between driving a car and riding a motorcycle is physically the same action of moving yourself from point A to point B, but the difference is in the act of observation. While driving a car you are encased in metal and glass and not subjected to the elements around you, but while riding a motorcycle you are a part of the elements and subjected to everything in the world. This is the difference between being asleep and separated from others and being awake and a part of the world as it exists today. I have already started you on this path by causing you to ask yourself several thought provoking questions in the previous chapters. We want to move from the concept of driving enclosed, to the concept of riding as a part of nature.

Note: When you are in this space you will start asking questions about information being shared with you, you will look at news reports differently, and your taste in music may even change. You will find yourself becoming less emotionally attached to them, but more emotionally attached to other things in the world. This is a natural part of the process. Don't be surprised if a movie or even a commercial, which has never moved you before, suddenly causes emotions to stir. This is natural in an awakening process.

When I was younger I hated wind chimes, they drove me crazy. Today I have a set hanging outside my office and I enjoy them immensely. I know if these chimes were given to me 20 years ago, I would have re-gifted them. I had a co-worker over for a BBQ one day, a "bigger than life" vampire, and the chimes drove him crazy. He is a big fan of low vibrational music with a lot of bass and angry words. I was surprised how crazy they made him, but I do understand why. It is that part of yourself trying to wake up, trying to be heard and I know he wants no part of it. So I took the chimes down for him, so he could enjoy his visit and our meal. This is what you become aware of, you see people's behaviors change, but it is not really their behaviors that are changing, but your conscious awareness of your behaviors changing. It is the fact that you are now consciously watching what they are doing. Returning to the car versus motorcycle analogy, you are hearing the words and watching the actions, you are not just encased in the car with the radio blaring and AC blowing, you are in the world with the wind blowing through your hair. So what does this say about people who "have to have" a convertible? Where are they in the process?

Before a child learns language they learn to observe and mimic others until they are told "do as I say, not as I do...." The act of observation has the potential to being more powerful then communication has ever been, poker players know this and so do intuitive people. They have learned to have a heightened sense of awareness by using the powers available to them through observation. The differences are in how you apply it, where a poker player uses it for something very specific in their career, there are others who have learned to broaden their abilities to see things or be aware of insignificant changes most people would miss. Many of us have forgotten that we learned an entire language through the act of being immersed in observation. It is a beautiful thing to have the skill of language in order to communicate, however, by using

53

language we have become lax in our art of observation. We have not only learned to communicate, but have also learned to use that language to deceive others. By flexing your observation muscle you can become efficient at detecting those who would use words to deceive you. It can be used to help you detect and discover many other types of deception, also.

The art of faking it involves becoming a master at observation. It is through observation that you will be able to determine deception through the actions of others. You will not need a lie detector or need to wait for the results of something somebody has said, instead you will know just by listening to the words being said to you and trusting yourself to know if it is the truth or not. When you say to yourself, "Something does not feel right", it is an indication that there is more to what you are being told. I think it is important to understand that many times this is not lights and sirens and it can be something very subtle that you need to really be watching for. It is not a party trick either. This activity can be extremely difficult, especially when what you are hearing from inside yourself is something that you really do not want to believe.

I always enjoy watching professional poker players because the best poker players in the world are masters at observing the actions of others. They do not put a lot of stock in the words said by other players, unless they can determine that the act of talking is in fact the action they are looking for. An example of this was a championship match where two players were competing for a large number of chips. The one player started speaking to the other player and this player had been quiet through most of the telecast. During this hand the quiet player started to talk back to the more experienced player and the next card was dealt. The exchange continued and the young player continued to talk becoming more animated during the hand, but in a very subtle way . The older player, faced with a large bet, looked at the younger, listened, and watched the younger player for 30 seconds or more and said "so, you have a talking hand, huh." This was all he said, but it was at this point that both players and everybody at the table knew that the young player had a very good hand and was broadcasting it by his change in habit. In this case, the act of talking was the action the other player was watching for. It was not what was being said, but the act of talking that convinced the seasoned player to fold his hand.

If you are going to stay awake it will be crucial for you to be able to observe and assess through observations without the confusion of language or words that may be used to distract you or illicit an emotional response. Consider that if another person has gotten you angry or upset, they have already achieved their goal. To cloud you and make it harder to hear that eternal child. Further when I reference god or God, pick a specific gender, or touch on taboo topics I am also seeking a response from you. I want you to use this book as a tool to identify what is causing your emotions to turn on, then I want you to be brave enough to ask "Why?"

For the vampires out there trying to master the art of deception it will be easier for you to spot and avoid these situations, as time goes on. The number one way to spot them is to compare their words with their actions. If the words and deeds do not line up, you are being deceived. For the more masterful vampires who have lived off the art of deception they are harder to spot and they are on the lookout for you. If you have ever worked with someone who keeps you at arm's length, shifts the energy in the room when you approach, or is aggressive to the point of getting an emotional response out of you, then you have met someone who knows you cannot be easily fooled with words.

It is important to remember at this point you goal is to become aware of these activities, not to try and fix them. You are working on yourself, not trying to fix the world. Confronting someone with your new knowledge will only force them to change their tactics. It is better to observe the tactics being used and sharpen your skills at detection. I will say this one more time. This book is not about waking up the world, it is about your personal awakening process. In this step you are becoming conscious to the world, opening your eyes and comparing words to actions. Courage and bold actions come later, for now, watch and listen.

Before the end of the year 2012, I contemplated several things that might be viewed as world changing and would cause a significant shift in those asleep: as well as those awake. I thought that one way to awaken more people would be to have a flying saucer come out of the sky, the doors would open, an extraterrestrial would come out and in a thick New York accent would say, "How you doin?".

At first I thought this might cause a significant shift in people's perspective and along with it their belief structure. It would make people think about what it is they have been told to believe and

55

maybe then a re-evolution would not be an *"if"* it would be a *"when"*. For me this would not dismiss the premise of there being a God, but instead introduces the idea that he had more than one laboratory. It would also help us realize that we are ALL humans regardless of the color, continent, or belief structure we currently have. We are a race among many, not the only "humanity". The more I thought about this the more I realized that the fear and division among our species is already to great for this event to cause anything other than more division and fear.

The other way the end of the world could have occurred in 2012, and I really liked this option, was if when everybody woke up on January 1, 2013; no one had the ability to lie without the person they were lying to being able to tell they were being deceived. Let's say a big blue light appeared above their head any time the person lied. A great movie, titled "Liar, Liar" told the story of a lawyer faced with something very similar to this. Now think about that, a world where every question has an honest answer, a world where the concept of using language to communicate deception is something a person cannot do. Politicians and world leaders, community leaders, and every person would have to tell the truth or remain silent for fear of the "blue light special". Deception has been rooted into our society at a very young age and is pervasive through every level it. The ability to get rid of deception is something that we can only do by observing with great intensity or eliminating the ability to use language altogether.

Guess what, it has already started and you are learning it right now. Learning the skills needed happens over time, but also intensifies the more often you use it. The exciting thing for many people who are awake is that they can see through the deceptions of language and can tell when people are trying to deceive them or corner them. Of course there are those who are masters at deception, can tell you what you want to hear, and lead you where they want you to go, but only if you are not listening to that eternal child. This is the hard part, there are times when what you hear you want to ignore. It may seem "to good to be true", but you have to find out. The vampires will use emotion to cloud your observation and try to get you emotionally involved to lower your ability to see what is going on. If you have not yet mastered the power of observation you may fall prey to someone who has mastered the art of deception, take your time learning this skill it will help greatly in the future steps.

For a master of observation, or master of deception watching a person "faking it" is like watching a young child who is pretending to be asleep. They have not learned yet to close their eyes gently so that they do not squint. A person who is a master at deception will see you if you are squinting or your eyelids are twitching.
Today, to function within the confines of what society requires, you will be required to use the art of shape shifting or wearing masks. Psychologists say the use of masks can be a defense mechanism for the person, but I would add that the use of masks is also an attempt to hide the fact that you really are awake, but do not want to be found out.....just yet. There were many times in my career that I would explain to people close to me that "what I do at work, is not who I am at home." This is an example of a mask I used to use while at work to ensure those around me were comfortable, that I was "likable", and did not unsettle many of the vampires. An example of wearing a mask is I worked with a lot of huge sports fans, so while I did not wear the jersey on casual Friday, I still knew the scores and highlights to make conversations easier at work.
The art of small talk before a meeting has very little to do with pleasantries being exchanged and a lot to do with sizing people up before the meeting. To have an idea of the sports scores is settling to people, much more settling than saying "I think sports are barbaric and don't follow the team." A comment like this makes it very hard for everybody to get on even ground for the meeting. Mind you I am not saying there is not a time and place for this, just not if you still have not mastered observation.

A child learns to use masks very early based on observing others, especially parents who interact with a wide variety of people on a daily basis. The child learns that there are those you communicate with on one level and there are those who you treat on a different level. A child can observe this by how you answer a telephone call or carry a conversation with a neighbor. Again this is through the power of observation and when observing the behavior of guardians, siblings, and the community; a young child will learn to develop their own masks, so that they too may relate to the rest of society.
Take the example of a parent who takes hours away from the family to learn to play golf, but when the child asks if they had fun, the parent says no, that it is just something they "have to do". The child

57

had been told that golf was a game, but the parent is treating it like it was something unpleasant, it also cut into the child's time with that parent, and it was not fun?! What the child does not learn until later on in life is that while the parent had no interest in the game, the reason they learn to play golf is because the executives play golf and decisions are made on the golf course. For this person, it was beneficial to their job if they learn how to play the game and found a way to be invited to join those executives, so that they may have input in the decisions. By the time the child learns the whole reason for the hours spent on the golf course, they may be faced with the same challenges. They may look at it and from previous experiences say, "Well my parents did it that way." We learn a lot from observation and to reawaken yourself, you have to remember this art and begin using it.

The concept of shape shifting as a way to "fit in" is not new, however, with the use of the technology today you can appear to be anything, or anyone through the use of the Internet. Physical shape shifting is much more difficult because you have to be physically present to make the shift. It is very hard to say you are an excellent golfer, if your scores at the end of a round of golf is consistently terrible. The Internet has provided us a vehicle allowing us to reduce the gap between people globally. It has allowed us to see other cultures and to assimilate information faster than ever before, but it has also allowed us to be more deceptive because we do not have to be physically present. Shape shifting using our words makes it easy to be deceptive, but doing this in person, is much harder.

This is because in physical shape shifting, your words must align with your actions and this takes skill and a lot of energy. If not done correctly, those who are aware of their own *present moment* while being in the same physical space as you, will know you are lying because they are connected to their world and yours. The worse part for the liar is that those who are aware and advanced in their practice of this observation, will rarely make it obvious that they know your words do not match your actions. If the person you are attempting to deceive is a vampire…Well you may leave the conversation feeling very drained.

It is a risk being present with someone else on both sides. For this reason many people who wish to deceive others, will indeed thrive on the Internet. There is no physical investment and no interpersonal energy connection. I am curious what will happen to the dating scene in the coming years as going out for drinks or a movie is heading in the direction of Facebook and Twitter where a physical presence is not, initially, required to attempt deception. A 16-year-old can make herself appear to be a 30 -year-old as easy as a 40-year-old can make himself appear to be an 18-year-old. While lying is an old craft, the ability to shape shift and use technology to accomplish greater feats within social media has only just started and I doubt the impact will be limited just to social sites. Before the popularity of sites like MySpace and FaceBook, in order to shape shift a person could create new masks to hide behind, this is no longer necessary on the Internet. The Internet is the mask and you can design it to your own liking honest or deceptive; kind or cruel. Growing up if you wanted to re-create yourself you would have to move from one neighborhood to another or one job to another. Now, with the Internet, moving can all happen with the click of a button to create new profile with a new email address. This gives them the chance to wear a different mask or entertain themselves with being an entirely different shape, gender, color or nationality. It is technology with so much potential to close the gaps between cultures and bring acknowledgement of each other into the light, but has the equal opportunity to create a new illusion for individuals, businesses and even countries.

Another interesting aspect is that now technology can also be used to track a person's past by simply putting their name and a Google search. We love to announce things on the Internet, update pictures and post comments. We *like* to be known. So we can put a well-rehearsed version of ourselves out there so people can find out a lot about you before ever meeting you. The well-rehearsed you…. This form of deception has led to many people using the Internet to do a background check on those they meet on-line.

In a world where personal interaction was required when I grew up we had an advantage because we were able to use and refine our "senses" about people before getting to caught up in their masks. Now, when the first impression you get is the picture of a sexy shirtless body who wants to meet you. Well, that sense is usually dulled by another chemical in your body linked to sexual urges. Profiles are read, judgements are made and people are shifting into the character they believe they need to become for the situation. The point is to ask yourself how dull your senses have become to being able to detect the truth. The Internet is a great mask or cover

59

story for all of us who desire social interaction, but, ironically, it can fall short on expectations when the goal is to become more connected to your species.

Another good example of shape shifting is referring back to the movie "The Matrix". In this movie the idea of shifting from a life of being something you're not; too being introduced to the opportunity of becoming your "potential". The movie did a good job of laying out the characters journey, trials, his own disbelief and resistance. All the same things people go through on their journey to be self-aware. When I say you are powerful, it is not bullshit, but no one can make you see it, Neo.

This concept is not lost on those who watch this movie and are awake. Neo knows there is something more than what he is seeing, but because he pursues it so relentlessly he is offered the opportunity to "see" what it is that is eluding him. When he sees it, understands it, it is beyond anything he could have imagined. Welcome to the path of being self-aware. The interesting twist on this has the person learn that they are a slave to their technology or as referred to in the movie a "copper top battery".

The main character, Neo, is offered the opportunity to not only shift in his persona in his reality, but has the ability to shape shift into a "reality" foreign to his nature… The real world. There is even a portion of the show where the character Neo is plugged in to a machine to learn martial arts training. Following this observation he opened his eyes and said, "I know kung fu". It will not be that easy for the true seekers in this world and anyone who tries to plug you into your own self-awareness, is trying to sell you beach front property in a desert. The best any of us can hope to do is share our experiences and give you the opportunity to find the path.

Then there are movies like "Avatar" which had the potential to show shape shifting through the use of technology, rather than being a slave to it. In this movie, a person who is limited physically became unlimited through shape shifting. The movie went on to show how a person can take on different traits once the shift occurs and can begin to adopt some of the new traits based on that shift. I was really excited when I saw this movie in the first hour it did an amazing job showing the infinite possibilities a person has in shifting their mindset, and becoming awake, based on how technology has aided them.

Then the movie itself shifted away from these concepts. By the

60

second hour you were back to the old concepts of war, fear, and vengeance. This group of highly enlightened "blue people" who knew how to stay connected to the earth became warring tribes overnight. The second hour of the movie resembled old black and white TV shows of Cowboys versus Indians except in this movie, the Indians won. Unfortunately for me, the show lived up to Hollywood expectations. Sure it grossed a ton of money and was very entertaining, but when you look under the hood there were several things that were disappointing for people who were awake.

For example, if in the end the full power and energy of nature, you know that power that could shift a man's soul from his broken body into a new body, that power! If it had taken on technology and stopped it in its tracks, man would have had to made physical contact and negotiated. Instead animals attacked, people were maimed and killed and the audience was glad to see it. What does this say about us?

If man had become an observer of the true energy of nature, I believe Avatar may have become a legendary film. I know I am in the minority because others loved the film for its action and story. From their perspective I have to agree with them, but in most cases I can only talk about superficial topics with these same people, anyway. Avatar took people on a entertaining and mindless journey where they did not need to think, just be entertained. It then carried them to a logical high energy conclusion that made the producer a lot of money. Great accomplishment, good movie, and too bad.

This is an illustration of skills that can be learned through the art of observation and while it is science fiction in these movies; in reality the art of conscious listening and observation are skills that you will need for shape shifting, wearing masks, and becoming a master in these areas to allow yourself to be ready for the next step of re-evolution. Also, be aware that the reality you will experience will not be as drastic as the last outpost of human existence, but at times you may feel like it. When you do be open to the fact that there are others around you trying to do the exact same thing.

Intermission:

This is the point in the book where you are now sitting on a bicycle at the top of a very steep hill. So steep, in fact, that by looking down the hill you get butterflies in your stomach. Now is when you contemplate whether you want to take this journey or not. If you've never taken a bicycle down a hill where your common sense was screaming at you that "you know better", then I will explain the feelings you are about to encounter. As you roll the tire over the crest of the hill and gravity starts to pull you downward you will first hear the rubber from the bicycle tires start to whine against the road as you pick up speed. You will glide along at first, accelerating every second as your legs move faster on the pedals. Soon that rubber sound is replaced by the wind howling in your ears. As the wind noise increases; your legs are moving too fast to keep up with the pedals, so you put them out to the side. This decision disturbs your balance and you start to wobble. You are tightening your grip on the handlebars as they begin to vibrate more as your speed increases. At this point, halfway down the hill, your eyes begin to water, you can't really see the road and the wind in your ears becomes deafening. What is running through your mind is why you pushed the bicycle over the crest of the hill and did not sit on your brakes, but your pedals are a blur now. At the same time you are afraid of all of these sensations, you are also exhilarated by the rush of the experience. Then before you know it the bicycle slows and comes to a stop. You made it. The rest of this book is that 30 second trip on the bicycle down the hill. This is as close as I can get to describing what it is like as you start re-membering your eternal child.

If at any time you find yourself getting emotional or off balance, think of this analogy of the bicycle and step on the brakes. Never let the pedals get ahead of you, tap on the brakes and take breaks when you need them. To allow emotions to run your thought process during this part of the book is the equivalent of taking your hands off the handlebars during that downhill ride. Would you take your hands off the handlebars? Then don't let emotions distract you from contemplating the words you put in front of yourself. You have made it this far.

Be mindful that it is my goal to stir shit up for you. If you only ever stay in the place that you know, where you are comfortable, then your will never evolve. If the rest of this book angers you or you find yourself emotional about what you are reading it is important to ask yourself why you are emotional and what perspective you are bringing to these pages.. This is my goal and honestly it is why you are here too. You and I are seeking, but something brought you here to experience my perspective. Congratulations, you are in for the ride of your life which is how it should be for everybody. My advice at this point is to hold on to those handlebars, keep your feet ready to brake if your emotions cloud your connection to your heart. And listen to that voice you have inside of you. For you die hard Matrix fans it is time to take the red pill.

Ok!! Intermission is over and I am certain all the zombies have left the building!!! Now the fun begins for all us vampires.

64

Parents

Let's start with parents…I will take this opportunity to thank both of my parents for all they have done for me….and to me. While therapy was never required in my lifetime, it is likely that it might not have hurt and maybe I could have come to some of these concepts sooner, however, it would not have been as fun a ride. THANKS! Now this may seem like an odd place to start after such a fun filled intermission, but consider this. Parents are people we all have had to deal with. Maybe not the traditional parents, but we all had teachers, mentors, or guides who parented us along our path. So before you decide to skip over this section because you are too young to be a parent, have already been a parent, or have no intention of becoming a parent consider this saying "it takes a tribe to raise a child". You are a member of the humanity tribe, so you influence everyone you come in contact with, even if that contact is only eye contact or a smile. On this journey we are usually provided a couple of guides we like to call parents; however, these are not our only guides. Like it or not, you are a mentor, a guide and often a parent to those around you who are observing you. A parent is someone who chooses to dedicate time to a child's early life experiences and development, but there will be others who will be in a position to have a profound effect on a child's growth. It is best not to skip this section, so that when it is your turn to act as "tribe elder" you can provide perspective the child may have missed or not heard the first time around.

In most cases the parents are a young couple who have had life experiences and feel prepared to lead a little person through this human experience. In a book by Neil Donald Walsh titled "Conversations with God", he described a point where it would make sense for the elders of a culture to raise the children and for the young to bear those children then turn them over to someone with more wisdom than they have gained in their short lifetimes. I had real issues with the idea of young people bearing children and then saying "here you go" to their parents as they ran off to enjoy their youth. See how my perspective twisted what was said. Part of my problem with this is emotional for me because my youngest child is now 16 years old and honestly when I heard this idea my reaction was "Wait a minute, I have put in my time". I am sure I am not alone in that thought, however, when emotion is put aside, I do see

65

the wisdom in the concept of having those with more wisdom raise the youth of the society, but this does not mean the young couple walk away from the situation, it means they begin their training as a tribal elder to one day raise the children of their tribe. Wisdom does not necessarily always come from age, but it can always be twisted into something else by perspective.

These opportunities to shift our perspective provide the experiences which allow us to enhance our own lives without having to actually experience the "event". Remember the saying regarding walking a mile in another person's shoes. This is nothing new, so the greatest enhancements to our own lives , could come from those with the life experiences we can absorb from a different perspective than our own. Is our society setup to appreciate these lessons? To gain wisdom through perspective rather than needing to have the experience?

Remember, we have the ability to learn from each other and teach each other at the same time. I can only imagine all the things I could learn from you about your reality. If we would just tap the brakes on those emotions that cause us to hold on to past experiences and see the things around us that are being made available to us on a daily basis; wisdom would follow. How much time do we waste in our present moment, living in the emotions of our past? The emotions of the past of others?

There is something to be said for those who have made it to their golden years... Even if it only means they were able to stay on the bike all the way down to the bottom of the hill, the point is they made it and probably have some worthy advice for the child at the top of the hill.

The scariest thing about parenting is that the child does not come with a book on how to engage all aspects of the new life you are holding in your hands. This is true of every child and every child develops differently requiring that you rewrite the book on how to raise the next child. Hence the reason there are so many different great books on how to raise a child, but the trick is to get a hold of the right book, based on your child. That can be tricky!

Let's focus on the first child in a young couple's life, the young parents are now holding this new life in their hands and they need to decide how they are going to approach raising the child. They either decide that they did not turn out that bad and will selectively follow in the footsteps of their parents; or they decide that they were

66

good people in spite of their parents and they were going to do things their own way. As parents, we act as models for the young life we have made ourselves accountable for, but we all seem to make the same single mistake from the very start.

With my girls I used to tease them when they were younger and tell them that "I had dug a couple of holes in the backyard and that no one would miss them until they turned 16 and since I had something to do with them coming into this world I can also have something to do with them leaving it!" This was a standing joke in our family for many years, but the root of this section regarding parenting is the idea of ownership.

The idea that a newborn child is "ours" , did you catch it "my girls" in the previous paragraph. This is the start of a mistake that many parents, teachers, and societies seem to make. We as parents do not own those lives, but we are simply guardians and guides for the experience of these lives until they are wise enough to guide themselves. So how do we guide these young lives to hear the voice inside themselves? How are we teaching them about their brilliance? We did not get it when we were sent to day care or learn it from the first day of school where I was, how about you?

The other part of this challenge is the outside influences that not only affect the child, but also affect the parents of this young being. These influences for both the child and the parent will include input they receive from friends, teachers, other parents, television, and the Internet.

Ownership is a natural feeling to have when you leave the hospital with your child. After all it has been your experience, for example when you were 16 you got your driver's license, then you got a car with a title and registration. You took the car home and took care of it so it would continue to run. When you became accountable for this young life you were handed a birth certificate and other documents with your child. The only difference in this process was the baby lost the "new car smell" much quicker.

There is no denying that the parents are accountable for their child, their behavior while they are young, and their well-being for many years of their life. The problem with looking at it from the standpoint of ownership is the transference of accountability from the parent to the child. Many parents believe that this young life is ultimately a reflection on them and the job they are doing as a parent. For this reason transference occurs to the parent who will feel an increasing

67

pressure to produce a "good child", so then a parent will place this stress back on the child.

In a standup routine by Bill Cosby titled "Bill Cosby. Himself" he stated that all children are brain-damaged and went on to explain several reasons why children are brain-damaged. From what I have seen in the troubled teens I have talked to it is evident to me that there is nothing wrong with their brain, instead they are blind to their eternal child and no one has taken the time to teach them how to hear their internal voice or even that there is an internal voice. It is very hard to hear this voice through fear and emotion.

Remember a time when you were trying to reason with a child or someone who was emotionally charged or upset. Yelling was pointless, it just made them more upset or worse it completely shut them down.   Reasoning with them did not seem to help because they were not listening, they were clouded by the emotion they were experiencing. Of course they were not listening, they were upset. How can anyone "hear themselves think" when they are upset.

Tony Robbins uses some great techniques to "distract" the emotional state. He uses "shock and awe" where the person is so shocked by what Tony said that they forget, for the moment, their emotional state which in turn gives Tony the chance to insert a critical thought. He also uses silly human tricks like burping and summer saults to clear the mind of emotion long enough for a thought to get in. The mastery of mentoring here comes from the coach's ability to listen to the seeker and see their perspective. Knowing how to use what the seeker is saying to guide them to the place where they can answer their own question, not be told what the answer is can be challenging.

To me this is paramount not only in life coaching, but in all aspects of guidance. A person already has the answers, even a very young child. They already know the answers to those things they are emotionally challenged about, until the parent comes in and tells them different. Then the child is confused....

Our job is not to tell them our perspective of the truth, but instead to help them realize their own, then they will own it. We do not "own" the next generation of humanity, we simply guide them to realize their truths, not to have them relive ours. So often we want to fix our child's problems, but we need to resist that urge and instead take these opportunities to help the child hear for themselves the answer. If you really want to screw up society, spend your life as a parent

68

trying to make your child's experience "better" than your own. Shield them from conflict and competition, reward them for nothing and allow them to ignore the work required to hear that internal voice. Then in your golden years you will reap a society of people who are exactly what you desired to create.

Every generation looks at the next and shakes their head in wonder, surprised that society has not completely destroyed itself. I used to listen to my grandmother complained about how "parents these days don't understand" and now I listen to my father say the same thing about our generation. He has stated more than once that he would be involved with social services if he had to raise a child in today's day and age and I believe he would be right. The concept of a *timeout* is a waste of time, in his opinion. He had other behavioral adjustment tactic for a young child. I can tell you that if I was put in "time-out" I would have LOVED IT! I might even be inspired to repeat what got me there in times I wanted to avoid something else. For me the threat and occasional use of a leather belt kept me out of trouble, but this was the book on "How to Raise Todd", this was NOT the same book needed for my other five siblings. Here again the idea of there being a profound truth in more than one way is the struggle parents deal with while determining how to best raise their child or children.

The two greatest tools a parent has to reach their child are the love they have for the child and the ability to communicate with the child without the need for words. The act of listening can be the most powerful communication method a parent can use with their child. This method of communication is very active and requires that the parent truly comprehend what it is the child is saying rather than believing they understand what the child is going to say and telling them how it is going to be solved. Niels Bohr once said "…the opposite of a profound truth may well be another profound truth." While parents strive to teach their children the lesson, what is profound is the fact that what the child is trying to teach the parent about the lesson may also be very profound, if the parent is listening. Many times the parent is so busy guiding and teaching that they are not listening and this is a profound limitation to the art of language we have grown accustomed to using in our society. There is no doubt that the parent will guide the child around many of life's pitfalls and sand traps, but if we look closely; the child can also guide the parent through past experiences which need to be healed,

69

pitfalls of parenthood, and mistakes they are repeating that their parents may have taught them. To be a parent is to take accountability for guiding and also being guided.

So the first step to reaching the eternal child, within your child, is nonverbal communication. This again is observation and active listening. Now the next step is what you feed your child. I am not talking about food here, I am talking about a walk in the park, time spent with your child skipping stones, or going for a bicycle ride. Finding ways to feed your child emotionally and help them learn to listen to that quiet voice inside of them. I can still hear my father yelling "turn off the boob tube and go outside!". The problem was I would go outside and there was nothing to do. So I would sit behind the woodshed at our house and listen to all the sounds in the neighborhood. I could hear the kids playing basketball, the girls riding their bikes through the neighborhood, and the neighbors arguing. At the same time, I started to hear that internal voice that has helped guide me out of trouble most of my life. There have been several times where my life could have gone down a very different path if I had not listened to the voice.

One of these times was while I was in the Army and a buddy of mine and I were coming back from a night out on the town. We had both been drinking, but only one of us had been drinking a lot. Unfortunately, I was also driving that night. As we walked out to my car and my buddy asked if I wanted him to drive. I told him we were only a couple of miles from the base and it was my baby, so I would drive. The walk to the car was not that far, but it gave me a chance to think about what I was going to do and it was not my logic or my ego whose voice I heard in my drunken state. Before I knew it I was standing over the roof of my car getting ready to drive back to the base. I made it a rule to never let anyone drive my car, but my buddy could tell that I was thinking hard about something and asked again if I wanted him to drive. I tossed him the keys and climbed into the passenger seat mumbling something about this being "stupid" with the base less than 5 miles away. When I got into the passenger seat I was sincerely irritated with that voice as we made our way back to the base. When we pulled up to the gate the military police were pulling people over and testing them for driving under the influence. At this point, I learned a couple of very valuable lessons. One, that voice, even when drunk can be heard if you are willing to listen. Number two, listening to that voice can be irritating.

It does not care about your ego or your emotions and will talk right past your logic. It can be hard to listen to, but you will feel that you should listen. When you don't it can have a profound impact on your life. How many times in your life have you caught yourself saying "I knew it!" or "I knew better." How did you know? You just did. And that my friends is the quiet whisper of your eternal child.

The goal here is for the parents to learn how to teach the child to "turn off the boob tube of your ego and to listen!" The best way to do this is to lead by example and be willing to listen, actively listen to the child, and then ask questions not dictate solutions. Offer the child every opportunity to hear and trust that voice. Again, by doing this the parent earns an ally within the child that will keep them safe, while raising the child to deal with the challenges of society.

Remember, that spark within all of us, is not a child. The experience you are having with that little person is a brand new fresh experience for them, but they carry with them a spark that has been here since the time of creation. Acknowledge it. It is there to also protect that new life. If we can teach children to listen and trust that voice then when the time comes that they are challenged by life, they will always have someone with them looking out for their best interests.

Knowing the little person has the option to listen to the eternal child within them and that this voice knows some profound truths seems to make it a priority for parents to introduce the child to the spark within themselves. Is this how the majority of parents raise their children? Or are they told what to do because the parent knows best?

Before you know it there will be outside influences surrounding the child they will begin making choices about friends, games to play, and the silly things that all children do; maybe even racing a bicycle down a very steep hill. If the parent has taught the child how to hear their inner voice and listen to the guidance being provided then the parent will have additional support in their effort to raise the child. It is important to understand that a child needs to comprehend love and how to access that love not only from their parents, but also from themselves even in times of emotional turmoil . This is the first step a parent takes to ensure that their child, while still a vampire, learns to move forward to re-evolve and not backwards into a zombielike state.

As the child grows they become more independent and make more

71

decisions without parental guidance. Even as a young child here are hundreds of opportunities to make a wrong turn. When they do, most parents asked the same question "What were you thinking?" According to Bill Cosby's theory, the answer given by brain damaged children is always the same; "I don't know". If I had driven back to the base that night, I have no doubt I would have been arrested. My platoon sergeant would have asked me what I was thinking and I would have had to say "I don't know." Fortunately, I listened to my inner voice, spark, soul, conscience, or whatever label you want to put on it. It is never to early to encourage a child to build a relationship with this awareness within themselves.

Being disconnected from the ability to have these conversations is a red flag for the parent and indicates that they should be concerned because the child is disconnected from themselves. They have no internal guidance system to help them when the parents are not around. In fact the truth is what they may be using is only their brain....Or only their heart and you really need all three. You tell me what is the third in this trinity? See you already knew......

As guardians, mentors and parents of our youth today our first priorities should be to dismiss the idea of ownership, put the ego aside when being concerned with how the actions reflect on us, and enable those guidance systems for the children to help assist them through their entire lives. The eternal child inside of all of us never dies it is simply ignored or cannot be heard over the noise and junk mail created by society today. Your job in this step is harder because now you must wade through all the noise you have learned from childhood and find that voice. This is the more active part of your journey. Everything I mentioned doing for the child in this section, I am also suggesting you do for yourself. In many ways we are all still that child.

The struggle I see most adults dealing with today on the surface is related to ego. How will what my child is doing reflect on me and the job I did raising them? This is something the parents must get past because it is not their life. They do not own it. While they were there to guide and educate the child during the early years, the child was there for the parent for the exact same reason. How many children are disappointed in their parents? Why? Could it be because the parents refused to listen to the child when the child had something important to teach the parent? Active listening. The child is there to educate the parents with the trials of their youth. Were the parents

listening to the child's needs on how they should be raised?
Adults everywhere pass up the opportunity to allow a child to teach
them valuable lessons, they are so focused on being the parent and
having a positive impact on the youths growth that they stifle a
conversation or interaction which might have caused them both to
be awake?

For most first time parents you start with a stressful situation.
Everything you do with and for that child is oversensitive in nature.
You are more protective of them, you watch them closely and keep
them from making too many serious mistakes. Then the second
child comes along and things have changed for the parents they are
not nearly as protective and do not keep as close an eye on them
allowing for more mistakes to be made because how bad can it be,
right?

As the first child of a big family I can tell you that there is no way I
would have been able to get away with some of the things my
siblings were able to get away with later in life. This can be profound
for the parent if they have taught each of their children to listen to
that inner voice because the answers for each child may be
different, even if the situations are very similar. This allows the
parent the opportunity to learn the concept of multiple truths. So you
see being a parent requires that you are both Guardian and seeker.
Strong enough to allow the child to guide you, both teacher and
seeker, both the parent and the eternal child.

This is not easy for anyone who chooses to be the guide for another
human being who comes into this world. For one reason, we come
to the realization that the journey of that beautiful human being is
inevitably what they chose to make of it. They can listen to the
eternal child and walk down one path or they may choose a different
path causing them to experience a different life. For 18 years we
may have the power to influence, protect, or spoil them, but the
decisions made are made by the child when they have developed
enough wisdom to be called an adult. There is much discussion
around the appropriate age for someone to be held accountable and
I believe it is much younger than our societies allow these eternal
children to grow and become fully aware of themselves, but many
do not teach the importance of observation and active listening to
our children. In fact it is ironic that most of these lessons a child
needs in their young years, people do not take classes like
meditation, yoga, and "team building" until they are adults.

So, parents will teach what they have been taught then move the child into a school system that they themselves are familiar with, then the child becomes a part of the same society their parents have lived in their entire lives.

Those parents who are awake understand the unconditional love that they share with their children simply means that regardless of what the child does they will provide the energy of love to them, however, this does not mean that the parent needs to approve of the nature which the child has chosen to follow. It is hard for a parent to identify that it is the desire of the ego, not love, to go and "make things right". In fact, the eternal child and our unconditional love may require we stand back and let them do it on their own. Often this type of separation is defined as "tough love". Love is not tough; however, the ego of the parent can be and if the parent cannot silence the ego to listen to the inner child then all they know is love of the ego which is tied to emotions and clouds the person from experiencing unconditional love. Unconditional love helps bring a person back to balance which cannot be done by providing "things", but by going back to the roots and listening with your eternal child.

Teachers

I want to take this opportunity to thank all of my parents, teachers, siblings, guides, and children for the impact they had on my life. Unfortunately, most of us chose to remember the pleasant events because it was the unpleasant experiences that caused us to evolve. The same is true of our experiences with our formal teachers of education. The important thing to remember is the profound effect we allowed them, like those of our parents, to have on who we are today. I had teachers who convinced me to pursue life with courage and integrity, those teachers I held in the highest regard. It was not until years later that I learned I also needed to hold the bad teachers in just as high a regard.

I was a senior in high school, just starting the year and ready to enjoy being the "top dog" for a year. This did not last long. I was given a note to visit a guidance counselor one day, this was odd I had never gone to one before. During this time the guidance counselor informed me that I did not have "what it takes" to get into college and I would need to find a vocation instead. He wanted to

74

help me decide on some options, but this is not what I saw as that 17 year old. I left the counselor's office in shock first, then became emotionally enraged at this counselor, who did not know me, who I had never seen before, would have the guts to say such a thing to me. I did try to get into college, however, my grades were not what they needed to be, so instead I joined the United States Army and was offered a nice cash bonus or the G.I. Bill when I enlisted. I remembered what my counselor had said and decided that I would prove him wrong and get my college degree. You see without that perceived negative event in my life I may have taken the cash bonus and accepted being a part of society based on what was written on that piece of paper in front of my counselor. I said perceived negative event because this is how I chose to process it at the time. The counselor was….counseling and trying to help, but what I saw through my emotional state was someone trying to dictate my future. He was describing the fate decided for me by society, but was not the fate I determined for myself. I went to the extent of photocopying my college diploma, putting it in an envelope, adding a sticky note to it that said "You were wrong. Thank you." and sent it to the counselor who had ignited my eternal child all those years ago. Today I would not have said he was wrong. This lesson will become clear to you as you begin to realize there is no wrong, for the simple fact that there is no right. These are words we use to classify the state of something. We base that on our perspective, but we know there can be more than one truth. Head hurt? Good you need to get out of your head and feel this with your heart.

Consider that a child spends a considerable amount of time "learning" away from their parents. For a young child both TVs and movies also feed the human experience and provide the hopes and dreams of a young child's view of the world. While at first this thought may seem a little hard to grasp, consider the type of shows and movies we are watching in this day and age. When I was younger, the shows that my friends and I enjoyed watching were stories of superheroes which included Superman, Spiderman, Wonder Woman and other superheroes. It was fun to watch the superheroes while they were on their quest to help humanity. Who is helping humanity re-member the infinite brilliance with you that was crammed into the imperfect meat suit so that the being can have the opportunity to reunite or remember its' infinite brilliance.

75

Can you remember?
Last year, during Halloween as children dressed up in their favorite costume I lost count of the number of vampires and zombies which had shown up at my door. What I do remember is that the zombies vastly outnumbered the vampires. This is what we are creating as our future society. We have moved from superheroes searching for our humanity and purpose, to a life sucking force bent on draining us of our humanity.

Society and Superhero's

I have always found it interesting that the superheroes spent much of their time learning about their own humanity or trying to figure out how they could mask themselves to fit in. While these types of shows are still popular today they are not the front runners or the box office winners. Kids today realize not everyone can be bitten by a spider or come from a different planet, but they may be more likely to run into a vampire or be consumed by a horde of zombies. The truly scary thing is they are much closer to reality than they think. The TV shows and movies of today include vampires with the ability to have special powers that allow them to feed off of an innocent person and then make that person forget what has happened to them while healing the wound to cover up the event. How does big business treat an employee these days? What about a college? A hospital?
Our society is turning accountability for teaching and guiding our children over to institutions and those institutions are using technology to turn them into zombies and vampires. Storytelling and life examples in the classroom have been replaced by DVD movies and Internet access. Sitting for dinner as a family to discuss the day's events have been replaced by fast food, eating while updating Internet social media sites, and yes even parents texting at the dinner table.....And unbelievably texting the adult at the other end of the table. It is true the parents "not having enough hours in the day" because this is how they have setup their life with society. This is what our children are seeing and what we are producing as teachers for the next generation. It is ironic that we create the society and then get frustrated with what we have created. Think about some of the cultures that have flourished over the last 20 years.

When I really engaged my journey to stay awake and become a seeker, I was ferocious and could not get information fast enough, in fact, my first Reiki teacher shared with me that I was the first "student teacher" she had ever had in her class. This kind of shocked me because I did not understand then, but I have explained that concept to you already. The interesting thing is how I got on this path in the first place. This was not an enlightened moment of self-realization, hearing voices inside my head, or even a burning bush. No, it was related to being a cheapskate pure and simple. My wife was having back issues and my father recommended she go and have a Reiki session. I knew nothing about this at the time, so I did some research and I thought, "My father has lost his mind." Now realize, I was a diehard computer guy at the time and my world made perfect sense to me. I had dismissed the inconsistencies of religion or anything abstract to screw it up, it was either a 1 or 0, everything was either black or white and life….was good. So when my dad introduced this idea to us I was less than enthusiastic about any of it. My wife continued to have issues, even though she had been to see several different doctors, so I did some digging. The Reiki sessions were $75 an hour and I had a conniption fit right there at my desk when I was reading about what happened during a session! My dad had said that she may need 3 to 5 sessions with a Reiki Master to get her balanced out and get everything flowing again. So I was staring down the barrel of a $375 bill that was not going to be covered by any insurance company and it wasn't even a massage. Here is where the cheapskate comes in. I discovered that the same Reiki Master was having a Level One class that weekend and I could go to the class for $80 or sign up for the first 2 classes for $150. At the end of the second class I would be able to do energy work with others. So I figured this was a great way to save myself some money and do this "work" with my wife, myself. So this is where I started my journey and I got here by trying to be cheap, not by being inspired.

Guess what….My superpowers arrived! Or I guess I should say, they were always with me and I just did not know it. Like they are with you right now. This realization was bittersweet because now that I was awake I saw what was going on around me and my "life" was no longer without challenges, I was awake and not really thrilled about it. Then I decided that like other things in my life this

77

was not made to be easy, so I needed to step up and take this as far as it would take me. While devouring everything I could find about energy and the understanding of our selves I had several things cross my path. The first one that really tripped me up was a DVD called "What the Bleep". I watched the first DVD twice and it only further fueled the desire I had to learn more, then I watched the second DVD in the set and a gentleman started this DVD by discounting many of the statements made on the first DVD. I was angry, so much for being a balanced Buddha! Why would they do this? Why would they put contradicting information from this guy on the same set of DVD's? So I calmed myself and listened carefully. Anger was not the right emotion; confusion was the right emotion. This is where I learned the concept of there being the possibility of multiple profound truths in a single instance. The ability to be right based on perspective opened a whole new world to me.

Another DVD I came across during this same time was a DVD called "The Secret". Those involved with this DVD gave some awesome advice, incredible insights, and produced something for those who were ready to hear about what them was inside. The show is food for the soul, it is inspiring and energizing. Then someone decided to make it a motion picture and put it out for the masses. When I heard it was going to be a major motion picture I was not excited about it. I had hoped that when it was released there would be little to no attention drawn to it by the mass media. I was excited about the prospects of something like this being put in front of people who were trying desperately to awaken, but felt they were likely the minority. The fallout was consistent with the world of zombies and vampires, they fed off of this movie in the mass media. The movie angered many people and the Internet posted a lot of negative feedback because this movie confused people who were asleep. This movie was not "entertaining", it was thought provoking....It was not "a wild ride", it was a conscious ride. There are those out there who saw the movie and it had an impact on them, but they are quiet about how it is working for them, Why? Those who are awake and in the early stages of their journey are still needing to fake it because all of those around them who went to the movie with them were angry someone tried to wake them up, that is why.

Think of it this way, it is Saturday morning and you have two options. Walk into your teenager's room and wake them up early to start the day. The rest of the morning and into the day you have to deal with what you just woke up and drag them through the day's events. OR you could get up and start your day, wait for the teenager to grace you with their presence and they can handle the day on their own terms but everything still gets done. Consider that there are times when the zombies and vampires wake up and they will find you when they are ready for help, but if you go in and wake them up, well then you have a grumpy teenager on your hands that was not ready to wake-up.

If we are going to evolve our society it will take DVD's and movies like this to act as catalyst's and teachers in today's technology age, there will need to be more attempts to put this information in front of people to show human potential and find ways to deal with the teenager. Recently Tom Shadyac produced a piece called "I Am". This documentary is very similar to some of the previous work done and needs to continue to be put out there for folks who are trying to move out of a dazed sleep. It is not only documentaries with the power to do this, there are countless movies out there also. The message is just underneath the surface....You just have to be in the state of observing and listening to hear and see these messages. Be your own teacher and when you get angry about something that flies in your face and challenges your beliefs....You will know you are on the right track!

I am not asking you to shave your head or become something you are not; in fact the beauty of the world is your individuality. You be you. If that means jeans and a t-shirt then so be it, if that means a suit and tie, so be it. Each of these modes of dress makes the person feel, personally powerful in their own space. Now if you are dressing this way, or that way to impress others or convey power over another, then you have lost the point entirely. Many of those types of people have not made it this far in the book, but if you have.....Congratulations, now are you ready to act on it? Are you courageous enough to be yourself? Can you "Bring it"? Before you answer this question be aware of one thing. In order for you to truly "be you", you will have to challenge yourself to appreciate and accept the realities of others. You are a seeker; you are a teacher; to be both you must have the courage and be willing to be outside what makes you comfortable. Simply put, it means living your truth will require you to be dynamic in your understanding of it, not static like a zombie.

79

COURAGE…..BRING IT!!

C.S. Lewis is quoted as saying "Courage is not simply one of the virtues, but the form of every virtue at the testing point." So to move beyond "Faking it" you must be ready to put some skin in the game and approach this journey with both courage, not for defeating the world, but for inspiring yourself. It has to all start with you. As all the ocean is made up of drops of water, it is every single person who will eventually change the ocean of humanity and create the society we desire to live in. To be clear this does not mean you must be fearless through this step, in fact it simply means you will move forward despite the fear. Any coach you work with, any spiritual guide you consult, any motivational speaker you listen to all require one thing of you. The cowardly lion needed it in the Wizard of Oz…..And you will need it to go beyond this step. Ready? Again keep your hands on the handlebars you're picking up speed and those handlebars are vibrating a lot. Amazingly enough, so are you……

I have talked about the drawbacks of being awake, but let's talk about something cool when you are awake. When you are awake it is impossible to be "blindsided". This is the scariest thing to a vampire, too. When you are approaching your life from a position of unconditional love no one can get anything over on you. You can see through the game of a vampire to the heart of what is going on….Even if you do not see it in the moment it happens, you can see it when reflecting on those times in your life where you thought you were blindsided, your actions had prepared you for them even if it was unconsciously. In my professional life I was terminated from one job and honestly I did not believe it possible for them to fire me for having integrity and doing my job, but they did. I was so mad at myself for not seeing it. I could not believe I had been blindsided like that. Then when I got home and calmed down I realized that we had only moved into this new space five months prior and for

80

whatever "reason" I had not taken all of my personal items back to the office. A lot of my business contacts and personal things I would have wanted to keep were already at home. While consciously I did not see the specific day coming, there was a part of me that knew as many as five months before the event, that this day was coming. The point is, we have everything we need within ourselves to stay balanced, we already have the answers, and we are able to predict where we should go and what we should do for ourselves in the future. This makes vampires very nervous because at this point they are not hard for you to spot. Take the example of someone working for a big corporation. A person who puts in 65 hours a week to try and finish a project for the company and at the end of the day, when the project is a success the boss takes all the credit and gets the promotion or bonus associated with that project. The person who did the work on the project is not really sure what happened to them by the time the process is finished and when asked about it they will respond" that is just the way the world works". The vampire may be the boss or executive who feeds on the other employee who does all the work. However, in today's society there are many vampires feeding on the zombie masses and even less experienced vampires. Vampires like to be in positions just above where a majority of the work is actually being done. The zombie will go back to work, will put in another 80 hours next week, and continue doing their job to ensure they get paid. If the person in this example is awake and realizes there's something wrong with how that happened then they may make a point to correct this error, but their other coworkers will remain in a daze state while this person tries to wake up. While this person feels conflicted and tries to reason with coworkers about why they are so upset it is not unusual to have a coworker explained to them that they need to " not rock the boat", "be a team player", or" keep their head down". These are both great tactics for remaining a zombie and effective tools for you to use to avoid being noticed by the vampires. Now with this in mind consider how this fits into the model of your government. How hard it must be to maintain a balance to ensure people only get exactly what they need to avoid a zombie apocalypse or vampire uprising? What skill it must take to keep so many blind or asleep and maintain the status quo.

Keep in mind not all managers are vampires. Some vampires are your coworkers and these coworkers can be identified as vampires

81

by how they interact with you. They are there for you by giving you encouragement and support while suffering through the injustices of your boss. This encouragement may include advice that you need to speak your mind or write a letter to state your side and give your opinion, but really what they are doing is feeding on your emotion and your energy. In fact, a way to tell if this is truly a friend or if this is a coworker who is a vampire in disguise, is to encourage them to stand beside you when you state your case. A true friend will support you and be there with you if you ask them to; however, what you will find in some cases is that this person will be absent when it matters most.

So why so many "lost connections to our *"soul"*? Well, today theology is not cutting it for people and unfortunately, we have advanced the "technology man" to a point where when we do try to listen all we hear is noise....A lot of noise.....So much noise that we cannot tell which is noise and which is important. Enter the field of the Life Coach......This is an amazing field and an area where well timed questions can cut through the noise very quickly and cause conscious thought to occur. I am not talking about therapy for your ego. There are doctors for that, who go to school, get degrees, and spend years analyzing what makes the ego tick. No.... here I am talking about a person who gets you back in touch with that inner voice, the self. Coaching is amazing work and we have all had occasion to "coach" others by offering advice to friends, family, strangers, and even our enemies.....Though this is a different type of coaching because it usually has an emotional tie to it. Consider that if we give advice to our enemies it is often not really constructive, is it? Advice given to our family and friends also tend to be emotionally charged as well, this is why coaching is different than advice. So, why would you not want to offer your best advice or coaching to those you disagree the most with? People are emotional creatures, right? Consider that a coach is not invested in a person's emotional state, they will not feed it, nor will they deny the person of it, but they will question it.

Courage in this step not only requires you to know when to act, but to also know when **not** to act. I find each can be equally difficult. When you have mastered this you are ready for the next step, however, there are some major hurdles within this step that include religion, politics, and the understanding of wisdom. This step can take some time....For me I find myself revisiting this step often....

82

and then there are days I feel like I never left, be patient with yourself and remember it is a journey, not a destination.

I once had a co-worker who had a flair for the dramatic and was able to deflect hard questions and move meetings off task very quickly if she felt threatened or was being questioned. I watched this behavior for months and usually people wanted her on the team because she was good at her tasks, but would not ask her the tough questions in the meetings, to avoid the conflict. The day came where I was leading a project discussion and I asked her a hard question which presented itself through the course of the meeting. You could hear the air get sucked out of the room and all the energy in the room just intensified within each person. She said to me "I know you don't like me" as an attempt to throw the meeting off track and move me into an emotional retreat and away from the question I asked. I simply stated to her that while I had great respect for the work she did, she was correct, I did not care for her methods used to sideline the meeting and evade my question. This was used to deflect the attention and maybe even to gain control the meeting while remaining distant from the harder topics of the project. I also knew that she felt questions like this were a personal attack on her worth to the team, so in my response I addressed that first by stating my respect for her work, then shared my concerns. Your conscious observation of these types of events can make these potential events easy to prepare for, but it is only in those brief moments where you have the opportunity to lead with courage, think quickly, speak slowly, and create an opportunity for a shift in how a person acts. Now I could have taken this entire conversation offline, also. I could have avoided the conversation in the meeting and taken it into a one-on-one forum, but how do the other people in the room grow? This takes courage and you need to move into these moments with confidence as you gain more experiences. Consider that you can take these steps and allow for change and re-evolution or remain quiet and sit through another pointless meeting avoiding real issues that can be resolved quickly with a little courage.

Another experience while on this journey gave me the opportunity to watch a person drift in and out of self-awareness. They were so close to being able to remain awake, if they would just have the courage to take the step forward. This coworker joined with a group of managers in an effort to better the working conditions of our teams following some radical changes by the director of the group.

83

We knew, trust, above all else was critical to our group and for this to work we would all need to work together and be on the same page. I also knew that this person was the "spy" among us. Remember it is hard to deceive a person who is awake. In this case, rather than force the issue I waited for it to come to me. I felt the direct approach would result in her getting defensive and retreating. I knew in the first lunch meeting she was struggling with herself and was not at ease about more than just the issues at hand. I watched her closely as I weighed my options on how I wanted to proceed. All the managers knew she had a personal relationship with the director and had known each other for over 15 years. They were dear friends, so the opportunity for the director to use that friendship against her and the rest of the managers was very real. I felt she did not stand a chance in evading the director who was a masterful vampire. It was an impossible situation for this person, but I also saw her in step two of this process. She really wanted to do the right thing and really wanted to be awake. So what do you do? You can walk away from this group and this person, allowing you the option to "keep your head down" and save your job or try and help this beautiful soul to understand her personal courage. After the first couple of meetings it was obvious to me she was repeating everything being said during our meetings, but I knew this was a good person on the verge of being awake. I also hoped that by her taking back what was being said, maybe the director would wake up and change directions or talk to us each individually about how to make things better. There were several times this manager spoke with me about her struggles and she shared her challenges with me related to her personal relationship with the director. During every conversation I knew I had two options available to me. I knew I could have the courage and integrity needed to give her the advice she needed as a genuine friend. To do this I had to ensure I was absent of my emotional desire to shake her like a ragdoll and tell her she had to wake up. Knowing that this required my honesty and listening to my inner self even though my ego was screaming that I needed to duck and find cover. The other option was I could use her emotion against her and attempt to shut her relationship down by using fear, thereby protecting my job. As a vampire I would feel entitled to do this because she was "the mole" and using fear to leverage her position and responses she gave to the director about the group

84

conversations would also feed my energy. However, this would do nothing to help her wake up and may actually drag her backwards into the world of being a zombie. It is fortunate for me that she could not find her courage; with her help, I was invited to leave and the zombies won, feeding the vampire, and securing another corporate nightmare people will have to navigate their way out of one day.

Why is this good, you ask? Well it gave me time to sit down and finish this book. The funny thing is I am not angry with her or the others involved with this great experience, instead I feel empathy for them and know they would not understand what I was saying if I told them I expected them to do exactly what they did, but had great hopes that they would not. This is an example of the times when you have the option to step forward and say with courage the words needed for others to wake up, or to sulk back in your chair and accept the life for what it is.

Now if you step forward keep in mind that this activity is something very familiar to the vampires out there and they may view you as either a threat or "management material". They will watch you closely, so when you start down this path....

You can find courage and blindly charge at every situation, but that will not serve you or those you may be able to help. Instead, look at the situation as if you only have six shots in a gun. Plan precision with each shot taken, plan for conflict, but avoid emotional investment, acknowledge your anxiety, and expect frustration. There are ways you will learn later which will allow you to attach to the source while detaching from the emotion. Giving you the advantage to rise above the situation and develop an unbiased perspective of it. Remember it is possible to be the victim of multiple truths, so it is best to learn their truth first.

So how do you find that connection to the eternal child? Like stated before you can get rid of some of the noise, delete the junk mail, or find a way to inspire it. Essentially, you need to feed it. This can take many forms maybe you are in a yoga class, have taken a meditation class, or are seeking out some form of personal energy class. It can come in the form of advice from strangers or maybe by receiving some form of alternative medicine that is causing you to now seek answers while you stumble around in the dark. In this case, being in the dark is a good thing and I will explain more about that later.

Courage is necessary while you wander through this phase in the dark in an attempt to see glimpses of light and to move closer to being awake. I would caution you that the first few times you are successful at using this courage ; you will feel invigorated, you will feel powerful, and it will feel like something you knew long ago, familiar in a way. Consider that this energy, this feeling, may not be yours to have; you may have taken it from others in the exchange. You fed off of whoever you had the exchange with. If you feel no rush of energy, just an even balance of flowing energy, yet you used courage and were successful, you got it! You used your own energy and were successful at allowing others to maintain theirs. This understanding brings you one step closer to understanding the world of the vampire where your actions can make you appear to be "right", but it does not mean you are correct in taking actions resulting in others losing their energy to you. If the result is a rush of energy, it will feel amazing. You will want to experience the sensation again, so you relive it in your mind, but this does not have the same thrill....Instead, you tell someone else what happened and it regenerates the rush. If you're a good storyteller and get lucky you will get an energy investment from the person you tell. You will then absorb energy from the person you are telling and believe it is from the original experience. This is why gossip is so popular, also.

The goal is to move to move away from absorbing the energy of others, to a point where you can identify that you are using your own energy as it is being connected to the source through you. When this happens the energy will not be in a big rush, but in an even flow. This will matter to you as you learn not to anticipate a great rush of energy when you harness the courage to take the correct action, at the correct time, from the correct place.

Yes you are still a vampire, but the difference is, to a vampire with no drive to evolve, it does not matter how the energy is accessed only that they own it and can feel the rush. What you are striving for in the next couple of steps is to move away from the desire to be right; the essence of the energy you are seeking does not come from the act of being right. The energy of being right is a personal energy and is how, as a vampire, you will feed. The essence of the energy you are seeking is universal, not individual. It comes from the act of being connected and remaining connected which, in turn, requires you approach this from a place of unconditional love. You cannot do this if you are trying to harm someone or wish them ill-

86

will, even if they "deserve it". If this is where you are getting your power, you are drawing this energy from an emotion or another person and you are being a vampire. Let's say you pull into a crowded mall and start looking for a parking stall. You find one and a person cuts you off or steals your parking spot. What is your response? Do you honk your horn, give them the universal sign for being "number one" or wish them the greatest good? What is the difference?

The "fact" is they did something that was not "right" and you have every right to call them on it. After all they took something from you, right? A parking space, so now you feel the need to take something from them. What will you take? Not the parking space as they already have that….The only thing you could hope to take from them is their energy. You need to feel like they have been embarrassed for being such a shmuck, so you lay on the horn. If they ignore you and walk away then maybe you feel like you have embarrassed them enough. What if they turn around and point and laugh at you? They have taken more energy from you and now you are really mad. See how this can escalate and the fight for energy happens every day and in every interaction. How about you wave to them as you drive by and sincerely wish them the greatest good with all the blessings they bestow on others be returned to them in kind? I don't care where you are from, everyone has met Karma and she can have a wicked attitude.

I am a big guy, 6'4 and my brother is just as tall. One day we walked into a crowded Sam's club to pick up some items. It had been a long day at work and we want to get in and out. As we walked in we discovered that we were lucky because we grabbed one of the few carts left at the front of the store. Soon we began weaving our way through the busy store talking about the day's events and discussing what we needed to buy. We were looking at an item and both standing in front of our cart while deciding if we wanted to purchase the item. Suddenly we both saw our cart rolling backwards out of our reach. We turned around and there was a man in his mid-50's walking in the opposite direction with our empty shopping cart. He did not ask us if it was ours, it was obvious we were both standing on either side of it that it was ours, but he walked up, grabbed it and started walking away. My brother and I stood there in shock, both of us had a look of anger, then we looked at each other in disgust. Seeing the look on my brother's face and

87

imagining the look on mine we both started to laugh. We could have walked up and confronted the gentleman about his tactics. We could have easily intimidated the poor guy in 3 seconds into giving us the cart back. Instead we just laughed and no one lost any energy.....If anything we came out ahead. We had a "right" to go over and take the cart back, but it was obvious to us that he must have needed it more to make such a blatant move.

It is in our nature to feel frustration, anger, compassion and love. It is normal to feel frustration when someone cuts you off on the freeway. You feel justified for laying into your horn because they put you in danger. Be mindful that your response is where the energy gets spent. If you are frustrated then it is your energy being fed on by those in the cars around you. Are you giving away your energy freely? Do you relive the event of being cutoff in traffic, for hours? Feel the need to retell the story that night at the dinner table? Why? The courage to letting go of the energy is sometimes hard especially if you are feeding off of the energy while retelling the story. Sometimes avoiding the opportunity to feed off a situations energy is what it takes when doing the right thing.

So how is the inner child activated and the connection maintained? Good question....How is it? You tell me. Is it meditation? Painting? Lifting weights? Cutting the grass? Sitting in rush hour traffic? This is the self-asking questions and is up to you to answer honestly, however, it is hard to hear the answers with all the noise present in our lives. Start by turning off some of the noise. See how long you can survive without the it. Turn off the TV and dedicate some time to sitting quietly with your thoughts. No smartphone, no Internet, just quiet. Become observant of the noises around you. Listen and observe. As you extend your time, you become a conscious observer of your emotions. You can watch yourself get frustrated, you can observe the times you get angry and soon you can avoid them, if it is what you want to do. You will begin to see opportunities present themselves to you and it will be easier for that voice to be heard. Know that I am not saying an hour of sitting in "time-out". I do not want anyone to say "Todd I sat in my chair for an hour every day and it drove me crazy. I didn't hear anything!" This should be a place you find calm....If you have to start with 5 minutes of calm, before you feel like you are in time out, then 5 minutes it is! I can promise over time this exercise and the desire to practice it will expand on its own. You want the connection to yourself and to that

88

awareness. Start small, go slow and then maybe out of the blue a coworker talks about joining a yoga class, or there is a seminar someone invites you to, it could be anything which would offer you a path to extend that time and experiences. If you are observant, if you are listening you will identify them when they happen. During these opportunities other abstract things may be presented to you or maybe words are spoken that feel real to you. Here is where the courage comes in. An opportunity is given to you that you "feel" is genuine. Now the question is will you have the courage to act on it? This is in no way an easy task and your ego will give you 10 reasons "why not" at every single turn. This is how many people get themselves stuck in a vicious cycle, so there are those who specialize in silencing some of the noise, deleting some of the junk mail, and helping locate the personal courage many people struggle to find.

These are mentors, guides, parents, life coaches and anyone who is skilled at eliciting answers to questions from the eternal child and the connection to self that is being reestablished....It is amazing to be a part of that experience and is like holding that newborn child for the first time, when the rediscovery is made. Stay on the path to remaining awake and connected, but remember you will likely go back to sleep for a period of time to rest. I keep saying go slow and be patient. It is not because I want to build your frustration level, but it is because this journey takes a lot of work.....Many times I decided never to go back to sleep, but it happens from time to time. Not because I want to, but because the world has made it so damn easy to do. If you find yourself lapsing back to sleep it is ok. Be kind to yourself and remember these are habits that are rooted in you from childhood. When this happens to me I just look in the mirror and say "Gottcha!". You can either forgive yourself and keep moving forward or dwell on the mistake, get frustrated, lose more energy and remain standstill until you decide in your own infinite wisdom that you need to just move forward. The choice is yours...

Tough questions can be a slippery slope. The longer you search the tougher the questions will get. At times people will stumble into a tough question and that will be enough for them to end their journey for a while. One thing I discovered in my own experimenting was that I had to first disconnect any emotions I had to my responses. If the tough questions activated an emotion in me, I examined that first. These emotions are often old feelings. Hurt "feel bads" from

89

childhood. If my answers have emotions applied to them they tend to lead me down the path of asking "life crisis" questions. This distraction is a result of society and the institutions used in cultures today. Here it is; the identity of self that is brought into question. Why did I do things this way? Why do I have no support from my family and friends? Why is my boss so mean? Why am I always so tired?

It is not enough for a parent or mentor to know the answer; they must let the person have the opportunity to come to their own answer. I would take this a step further, by saying before you try and answer the question, what emotion is involved with the question and its answer. This is something no one can answer, but you. This is contrary to how we teach and raise children today. This method is accomplished by asking questions and the questions asked need to be addressed by the eternal child, without allowing the ego to get these questions wrapped up in knots. Those mentors of the world know how to disarm the ego or distract it long enough to go straight to the heart of the matter. Tony Robbins has spent his life tapping the eternal child of people and reconnecting them to their higher selves. He prefers "Life Coaching" as the title and is very good at what he does. Of course, he has many critics and he handles it with courage and stays his course, while following his bliss. He realizes that anyone can be shown the path, but he cannot walk it for them. Now, one thing to consider is where do these people go following their reconnection to self? Do they have the courage to move forward and remain awake in the world as it is? They do go back into a world of vampires and zombies and it is tough! You know this, so does everyone walking this path….. It is not any surprise that those who stay awake try desperately to find a way to become an entrepreneur or self-employed to allow them a little bit of breathing room from the zombies and vampires. Here is the beautiful thing, those who are successful at making this "separation" from the world actually use that separation in service to those who are still zombies and vampires. It is a joyful thing to understand. To be in a state of bliss and providing a service to those you want to help find their bliss even when you are faced with negative feeling or working through tough issues yourself. This is when you are actively listening, consciously watching what is happening around you, and still moving conversations with others through acts of courage. This is when you become familiar with your own "dark walker". More on

90

this in the next chapter.

One final, rather dark, thought for this section that you need to consider, as you are now screaming down the hill at maximum velocity on your bike. Imagine an individual who has been asleep their entire life, who has tried desperately to wake up only to find when they awaken.....society is really full of nasty people and oppressive energy. They come to the realization that many of those around them resemble vampires and zombies. While awake they become aware of the added fear produced from a world of media programming designed for the masses. If you look at the world, ONLY, through the eyes of mass media, what do you see? What do you think the zombies see? Most importantly they will understand that it was through their actions, or indecisiveness which created our societies and cultures?

Our social, economic, and political structures do not profit from people being awake. They can only prosper if the majority remains asleep and lives in the fear presented by mass media. So there are those people who do not have a place to ground and balance themselves, so they are twisting out there by themselves. They feel the drain of others around them and cannot find that eternal child or purpose, no matter how hard they try. What do you think the effects of this may have on people? How drastic are the measures some people may go to if they are that lost? Think about some of the interviews done of TV where a person who has taken a terrible action against the innocents of humanity is described as "quiet", "kept to themselves", and it just didn't seem like they were "the type". Most of them are not "the type", but humanity.....as of yesterday....IS! Why yesterday? Well because today you are feeding your eternal child, beginning to listen to that voice, and hundreds of thousands of people are starting to wake up, which really excites me.

These folks waking up have experienced enough of the material excess, the technology tsunami is receding, and the drone like sleep of their lives is becoming not enough anymore. Many have had enough of the society they created yesterday.

91

BECOME A DARK WALKER

This may sound ominous, but I promise this is nothing more than your ability to walk through the dark without the need to really see where you are going. You do this often in the middle of the night when you can navigate from your bed, around the dog, over the cat and into your bathroom without turning on the light. In fact the light is overwhelming and can disorient you if you flip it on, so a dark walker it is!

In this step you are beginning to hear the voice of your eternal child, you are beginning to connect to your source and retain some of that energy you had previously been giving away freely. You are a seeker, maybe for the first time in your life this label feels real to you. You have found something to be really excited about. You may still be a little skeptical and get frustrated from time to time, but wow there are so many possibilities and you are excited to "see" it all. The easiest way to do that is to throw some light on it. Do not be too anxious to turn on the light, you will blind yourself. You have been walking around in the dark for a long time, you have become skilled at navigating the areas you understand and you know where everything is located, so bringing in too much light, to fast, can also have negative impacts on your growth. It is better to allow yourself the opportunity to get used to walking around in the dark while bringing the lights up slowly to allow for your eyes to adjust. By this I simply mean focusing on things that will make that voice you hear inside you louder and strengthen the connection in your heart and your head, turn off some more of the noise. Here is a start. Turn off your car radio on your way to work, try and leave it off. The radio or music is a great distraction from the self, turn it off. Why is it so hard for you to be with your thoughts? This is why you need to remain in the dark for a while. The end goal here is not to become a masterful vampire, the end goal is to be awake and connected! To rush this process, would be like throwing the light switch on in the middle of the night and trying to orientate yourself quickly. This will result in you becoming nothing more than a masterful vampire. The one thing that all vampires know, is they want it now......their way.... One who is connected and awake understands that it is already theirs and that patience will create the opportunities for a much more fulfilling experience through this journey of life. The vampire takes what they want in the moment, loses satisfaction with it quickly and moves on to something else. This is how we became a disposable society. You see now, to be a dark walker does not mean anything ominous, it simply means you can see your path while in the dark. Leave the light off.....get used to your inner voice, feel the personal power you are generating and learn how to make the most of it.

A zombie? A vampire? Or an innocent who is on their way to becoming some form of scourge of mankind in the future?

Take a moment and really consider the humanity that we see in people today. We raise our children to be competitive, to be better at doing things than the other guy, and to be ready to protect yourself in bad situations. I know what people are saying "I did not create this situation it is just the existence that I have to deal with today." In many ways I cannot disagree with that perspective. As guides for the children we bring into this world, we must protect them from the humanity that has been created by our parents and their parents and continues to be the existence we perpetrate to this day. In the history of mankind, we have not yet had an entire generation which has based its existence on love, we are still a culture of warring tribes and self-absorbed consumers who worry about our own comforts and human significance. So isn't it time for our kids to learn more than reading, writing and arithmetic? I think the"3 R's" have had their day and are still important, however. How about we add in "3 L's" to teach our children about the connection between their heart, mind and eternal child. Love, Live and Listen. We add classes to teach them to Love courageously, Live Boldly, and Listen consciously. What type of world will that create for our next generation of humanity?

So, the next time a person cuts you off in traffic....wish them a safe journey and the greatest good for the other drivers on the road they encounter. Ever want to see a police officer appear out of nowhere.....This one has manifested for me several times. I just drive past them and smile thinking of the other drivers who have been saved witnessing the driving behaviors of the person now getting a ticket. Now, it does not always work this way and to "expect" it to happen that way is not really staying connected to the idea of the greatest good. It is important to be at peace with this process and rely on the fact that the greatest good will occur....whatever that is cannot be your concern, wish, or desire. Again, that requires an exchange of energy and is something you are learning.....Now you are learning that karma and consequences are better off left to the energy of the greatest good. Sometimes that happens to be a police officer that appears from nowhere.

Today we still value the "competitive spirit" above most everything else in our culture. We see this competition as a way to get ahead in our families, our professions and in our lives. We instill the value of it in our schools, our workplace, and even our commute to work. When driving to work as the car races past you to get one car in front of you then cut you off in traffic. How do you compete? What aspects of your life do you draw on for competition? Ask yourself what completion.... competition achieve for you while on your journey. Amazing how close in spelling these two words are, isn't it? Really focus on that question and try hard to come up with something that goes beyond your perceived significance to the material world.

We believe we have evolved, that we have become something greater than our past, but let's use the example of any competitive sport to support this thought. The very root of competition is the belief that one person or group of people is greater or better than another individual or group of people. Yet at the core of our being we are all the same, it is just the meat suit that is different. Every one of us has a part of self that is as brilliant as the sun, so how can you compare the brilliance of two rays of sun?

The answer is you can't compare them, you must become a human form to experience that separation....that individuality. So, our competition is based on our physical being which is also limited to a very short period of time within the span of our life, yet that part of us which never dies is equal in all ways to every other person. On the weekends, people gather in an arena and they cheer for their favorite gladiators. This may be football, soccer, hockey, boxing, or any other sport where there is a requirement for a victor and the defeated. This may also be in an arena in Rome, have we really evolved as a species? Okay, so we are not feeding people to lions, but we are still allowing genocide to occur on our tiny planet.

Let's stick with something easy to measure, during whatever sporting event we are watching we get swept up in the moment with the rest of the crowd. We become a part of the mob. We show our "support" for our favorite team by wearing team colors and cheering them on from the stands. We even use phrases like "my team is really doing well this year" or "I went to the game on Saturday and we won". When I hear phrases like this I am tempted to ask the person making the statements what position they play on the team. In the times I have asked this question I have gotten a confused look. Our energy is being attached to something we want to participate in, we yell and cheer when the team scores a touchdown.....and yell and scream when they fumble the ball......All that energy spent, and then after the game most fans like to find a place to take a nap. Why? You know why. All that energy spent needs to be recharged, so they either turn to other people to get it, this is the quickest way, or take a nap. Now how does this differ from the energy moving through a yoga class? Understand I am just talking about the energy right now, not the emotions tied to the energy.... This is discussed in one of the later sections. The energy itself is identical except one is tied to the personal power and the other is tied to the source. Remember energy, just is. It always has been, it always will be. It can travel; into, through, and out of form and we can manipulate how we use it. Part of this manipulation involves emotion.

We have looked at how to remain a part of society by continuing to wear the right clothes, buy the right vehicle, have the right friends, and being involved with the right people, socially. In this step it is important to understand that the person on this journey is often confused and trying to understand why society feels so different than how they feel inside, the disconnect. I once heard somebody explain that the physical form that you see in the mirror today is a manifestation of what has already been created. I would take that a step further and say the society that we are a part of today is also a manifestation of what has been created by our past. In this way we are moving ourselves to live in this moment, but our society is set on living in the past and feeding on emotions of things we do not live today in our present moment. This is why we feel a disconnect. As we wake up this will feel odd to us, it will just not feel right and we will not fit in. Imagine that.....Throughout our lives we were shown examples of people and kids who did not "fit in", but in actuality they were the ones living in the moment. They were the only one's who really did fit in. This is not who we have to be as humanity, but is a reality of something we were in our past. If you feel different inside, like the world around you has its' priorities messed up then you are not alone. You may feel like you are walking around in the dark, alone; however, there are more and more people you are going to start "bumping in to".   In fact, there are a growing number of people who feel the same way, and they will cross your path as they are meant to in the right time and space. Now when these groups start to get together there is something else to be very aware of and that is your present moment.

In your present moment you have the capacity to join a group and may gather to try and fix society, but what is this? This is a well-intentioned distraction from self. Remember you cannot fix the problems of society through laws or rallies. You can only do it by understanding the eternal child. By living in the present of solutions, not the past trials and errors. History has shown there are some very serious issues with trying to make a change too an established ideal or institution.

Remember the analogy of turning the light on in the middle of the night. There are those who just want to blast the light on and get it all "on the table", but people cannot deal with that and become disoriented, confused, and scared. There is nothing more unpredictable than a scared human being. A person can be secure in themselves and fear what they see humanity becoming or they can be secure in the ways of the world and fear their own significance, but to have a fear of self and fear of humanity has resulted in some tragic events. The question is how long will you stay awake given the fact that you now know you are not here to fix society, but to understand your own humanity? This will not help you wage a revolution against the society of our past, but prepare you for the present of your own re-evolution.

While moving about as a dark walker it is important for you to understand that there are various twisted forms of love in this world, the key is to recognize the other forms of love and begin to understand why they became that way. You can only do this if you can create a new perspective. What you want to learn to carry forward is the unconditional form of this love that will spark change for humanity. You will be that spark for society and when there are enough people living in the present we will get to a re-evolution point where the change will occur naturally, without effort or strife. We will focus on humanities greatest good for evolution and will find that we can transition into the present with relative ease. Those things we are made to fear, ridicule or take acts of aggression against will all fade. It is our job as dark walkers to help those trying to remain awake to have an appreciation for different ways of life, to learn to love, and allow the twisted forms of love to re evolve so they will return to their pure form and will include everyone unconditionally.

It is not in our nature to desire to cause harm to others, but instead is a learned trait through our society. This means that being a bully is not something that you're born with or aspire to be, it is something that you are taught by the society, the culture or the technology you live in and it is obvious in today's age it is not always the parent who is the teacher. It can be the tribe who inspires this activity, however, from the present we can change it. How many high school gym classes consist of a yoga class or an "inner self" class of some type? Nope they still play dodge ball and try to hit someone else with a ball to get them, out. But, there must be more to it, right!? It is by asking ourselves this question that we have placed ourselves exactly right….here. You are present.
Humanity has not witnessed the day that our children spend as much time learning about the love of self as they spend observing the material, political, or religious beliefs of their society. When they do the entire structure of the past will begin to dissolve and we will all be ready to sing a new song from our heart. This is when the institutions will no longer keep the masses asleep or the vampires in fear, which will be the time of great re-evolution and feel like a gentle breeze for those ready to make the transition to the present.

Religion

The scientist created man, but was it man who created evolution? Why would we need to evolve if god got it right? Or did he get it right and we screwed it up through our evolution? Tricky questions, huh? Makes it even harder if you take the sentence "God's will" off the table as an excuse. This evolution was not due to a mistake made by man, but because man had come to rely on nature in different ways through the ages. In this way man evolved its' needs from a reliance on nature to provide abundance and protection to the current forms of love man subjects nature too. Some call this love, abuse….Which is a twisted form of love, right? See how this works? Religion is the same thing. A spiritual belief is a form of love, but theology is a twisted form of that love because it changes with man. It will change based on society changes. Spirituality always stays in the present and consists of a faith in the greatest part of self and in the conditional love. Theologies have conditions and rules, too. So is one better than the other? I would ask how humanity will evolve before being able to answer this question. When you put yourself through this re-evolution you will be able to make even more excellent points as to why man's god is too limited

to be the scientist. A good illustration of this is a favorite joke of mine from an anonymous contributor that went something like this:
 A man was walking in the mountains enjoying the scenery when he stepped too close to the edge of the path and started to fall. In desperation he reached out and grabbed the limb of a tree. He was petrified as he assessed his situation. He was hanging about 500 feet off the floor of the canyon. If he lost his grip on the branch he'd plummet to his death.
Full of fear, he cries out, "Help me!"
 But there was no answer. Again and again he cried out but to no avail.
 Finally he yelled in frustration, "Is anybody up there?"
 A deep voice replied, "Yes, I'm here."
 "Who is it?"
 "It's the Lord"
 "Can you help me?"
 "Yes, I can help."
 "Help me!"
 "Let go."
 Looking around the man became full of panic. "What?!?!"
 "Let go. I will catch you."
 The man thought for a moment and then asked, "Uh... Is there anybody else up there!!
Welcome to your present....You are here now....You are on the bicycle going at the maximum velocity you can go....Your eyes are watering and the adrenaline is pumping, one twist of the handlebars will send you flying from the bicycle....
In this joke the man, has evolved his need for God as man has done with nature over all these years. Willing to listen to other options of greed and abuse and waste presented by big corporations as they became known to today's society as the ways of truth. What are your truths? Where did you get them? Do you have the courage to look them in the eye and examine them from the present? Did God speak to prophets, Apostles, or is he talking within you right now?.... Why are you so far into this book? What is vibrating within you that makes this feel like something you have been looking for? The other question...How have you allowed yourself to perceive what you have read so far? Do you see yet that the best part of God exists within you and speaks to you about your truth? Our human experience and ego must find a way to interpret that truth for you to verbalize, so we use the crude tool of language. If you can verbalize your core truth into language you will accomplish

something that has evaded me for decades.

This book is a crude attempt to help you reconnect with your eternal child. To show you that what it is you are hoping to learn from this book, is something you already know, but need to re-member....ReMember your connection to that eternal child. It is hard to put words around something which cannot be seen or touched. It is like verbalizing "faith". You know what faith is, but verbalizing the art of faith is hard to do.

In my faith I know there will be critics who will believe the paper used to construct this book may be better served as bathroom tissue and I appreciate their perspective, but view it as a view from the past. Then there will be those I know, love, and admire who completely disagree with how I have come to view the world. I appreciate their perspective as well, however, faith is understanding that each of these situations is perfect and that what was perfect for me, was ensuring I published this book for you.

What are your rules around religion and faith? When I was a child our "faith" had strict rules in the church regarding consuming meat on Good Friday, but over time that "rule" was loosened for those with certain conditions. My question to nuns, parents, and priests at the time was, "Why would God cause these aliments in a person and then create a rule that people could not adhere to?" I never did get a good answer to that one. Additionally, consider the use of birth control. Some faiths have completely removed the stigma related to the use of birth control, but still preach abstinence. So why remove the hard line on birth control if that was what was required of the faithful? Recently, another of the largest religions had a very hard line belief regarding homosexuals. They had been teaching for decades that this was not by God's design, but was a "choice" made by the person. They have recently changed this view, but wait....did God change the view? Was God wrong? Or was the prophet wrong? Or was it all wrong? Religions are having a very hard time with those who are waking up and listening to their eternal child.

It is glorious because we are re-evolving our need for god and our understanding of the social rules we have created for ourselves to live by. Many people are hanging on that proverbial cliff and asking if there is anyone else up there. Some will say that God has spoken to them and it is God's will to change the rules. Agreed, that source of all has spoken to us, it just takes some of us longer to hear the words then others. We all have the capacity to know what the source is saying to us right now, it is not a secret club, just a quiet one. You will know if the words in this book ring true to your eternal child, many words may make you mad as hell, but remember you are going too fast to take your hands off the handlebars now, you have to disconnect the emotion and learn to listen to yourself. What do you hear past the fear and anger? I know many people need their god and have always had an external entity tell them how to perceive the source, so to acknowledge that this lives within you means relearning everything you have spent a lifetime absorbing in a theology…..But to believe the source lives within us and talks to us is not something some people are ready for. They prefer to put that responsibility off on a prophet or priest, rather than listen to it themselves. It is like flipping on a light in the middle of the night. The experience will be blinding and disorienting to most people and they will experience a "cognitive dissonance". This is your word for the day….This is the minds conflict that occurs when a belief or perspective is disproven based on new information. Emotions can run high when this happens and those who are most asleep will look for ways to reject this new information. They will convince themselves that there is no conflict and believe (for all my "The Matrix" fans) that "There is no spoon." It took a long time to believe the world was not flat and that the earth was not the center of the universe, but for every person to come to realize that they are a part of it all and central to it all. What will that take?

So now that we have walked in the dark for a bit you are ready to turn on the lights, right? Again, do not be in such a hurry to get nowhere; this is the journey and you will not reach a destination. This is not a race and you will not reach a finish line and be handed a trophy that says "Enlightened".

There is so much to explore and appreciate about theology. For many people this is how they have spent their whole lives, this is how they have been taught, about faith and how their culture raised them. To believe you are a part of something greater than yourself and that there is purpose to your existence, even if you come to awareness that the purpose is to experience the existence, not to have a predefined role…..Well, it is a divine feeling either way, isn't it? Why does one truth have to be right? I could never find peace in catholic schools because there were too many holes in the teachings and when I questioned it I was told I must have faith. When I was young, my parents dressed me up every Sunday and marched us all off to church where we would endure an hour of Roman Catholic ritual to learn….faith. I can remember listening to my parents say the same thing every Sunday, but was struck by these words of the Nicene Creed "*We believe in one God, the*

Father, the Almighty, maker of heaven and earth, of all that is seen and unseen". It was not the words so much as the droning of the them from my parents and those adults around me, like in a trance. Could this be a form of meditation? A mantra?

Being privileged enough to attend catholic school for 12 years I had the opportunity to also learn the creeds, prayers, and proper ceremonial responses through my teenage years, but became more skeptical because the more I learned the less consistency there seem to be around a theology I had spent every Sunday being a part of. Not to mention the quite voice telling me that there must be more to this idea of faith. Life could not just be about believing there was a score keeper sitting on a throne with a desire to see if I will fail. Then when I do and I know I will because I am a sinner, to be judged by the scorekeeper who created me as a flawed human being and given impossible rules to follow. Nope, there has to be more to it. Enter the understanding that other faiths exist. So why was mine better? Or at least why was what I was being taught, right?

I began to have opinions and asked questions about why the bible said one thing, but we practiced another. I was a child and was quickly dismissed by the adult who would say "well you just need to have faith." If I could offer a small tidbit of advice... Don't dismiss questions from a child so easily, they are closer to their inner child than we have been for decades. They are not a group of young people who should be seen but not heard. When they speak, I always try to listen consciously.

It took me decades to understand my frustration was not with my inability to have faith, but in my inability to follow a theology where the definition of faith was not consistent with the actions of those claiming to be faithful. I have observed too many Sunday afternoon parking lot episodes where a person who had just shaken hands with another while in church was then cutting them off to get out of the parking lot faster. The symbol of peace demonstrated through a handshake less than 15 minutes before was now the blare of a horn and the universal hand gesture which did not mean "you are number one". Needless to say my desire to attend Sunday mass changed when I was able to drive and I made the decision, after being schooled for 17 years and had partaken in the Sunday rituals for just as long that this was not all there was to having faith.

The child's definition of faith is much simpler yet so much more profound because in this process they base everything on love and the love is unconditional. It is very simplistic, but all-encompassing and it is here where you begin to understand a child is a guide to their parents and tribe, also. You see a child would share an ice cream cone with a dog or a friend with equal enthusiasm until interfered with and taught "to know better". Fear is what is taught to the child….dogs have germs and friends have germs, so don't share, don't talk to anyone you don't know and unconditional love goes out the window, but is a beautiful lesson for us parents while the child has it.

Following unconditional love, fear is the first lesson taught to a child, usually in the form of the word…."No". The child will follow a parents lead based on the faith they have in them, not realizing that the parents themselves are living in the fear learned from their parents.

It is a great joy to watch the energy of a child playing on the playground. It brings a smile to my face and wonder to my heart, as I watch the child openly share the energy with the other children and they begin to interact in a natural way. Unfortunately there are times I have seen children playing together without any concern of the world around them and a parent calls the child over to them while they are playing with a new friend. In this case, what was observed was the new friend had a darker color of skin, what followed was crushing to see. I did not hear the conversation, but it lasted less than two minutes and when the child returned to the playground the young soul walked right past his new friend and found another playmate. Lesson learned. Love was crushed and fear reinforced. I wanted to walk over and shake the adult into seeing what I saw, but that would end up with me spending some time in jail. Then I thought I could have a civil conversation, but knew from the parents reaction that this was pointless. At best she would tell me to get lost, at worst she would tell me that "This was her child and she would raise them as she saw fit." In either scenario I would have ended up in jail given the laws of our society today and the "rights" of parents to be mentors to new life.

I could see both children were confused and you could see that neither really understood because in their heart there was nothing wrong with associating with another human being. At this point, it is the parent who should be learning from the child. This is true for adults also; we need to understand that our greatest teachers may well be our children. For me it ruined my experience of joy I was having and I decided to leave.

Consider this example. A child walking down the road finds a bird with a bent wing and feels compassion for the bird, scoops the bird into her hand and continues to walk to road telling the bird it will be ok. The two of them sharing compassion and love for each other. The bird calms in her hand and the child cups the small bird to keep it safe from the bright sun and predators. The child arrives home and opens her hand to show her mother. The parents reactions can be numerous and will impress future actions for the child based on how they respond. What would your reaction be?

The first reaction from the parent may be that of anxiety as the child opens her hand and the small bird senses the change in energy and flies away. The mother then rushes the child in to wash her hands, telling her about diseases and how nature is dirty. Mentoring her that there is a separation between nature and man. The child may not help heal another creature for decades or for the rest of their lives. The child will be taught to feel powerless and be subjected to nature instead of a part of nature. If the mother were to approach slowly and comforts the child and bird, would the outcome be any different? How do you know? Or do you just have faith? Will the child begin to see the unlimited potential they hold in the palm of their hand at such a young age? I think so.

It is not the child that understands the themes of hate or violence or bias, until another teaches it to them.

In eighth grade I was extremely confused about my place in the world and about my faith. Parents, teachers and priests told me to have it and I tried, but I also rebelled. Every week someone in class was chosen to read a passage from the Bible and then the class would discuss it with the priest of the parish. I was chosen to find a passage to discuss and then explain why I felt it was significant. It was horrible I had no desire to be dragged to center stage, but looking back I think this was an attempt to bring me into the fold and curb some of my youthful animosity. Instead, I found something that gave me hope and I wanted to discuss....

Matthew 6:1-34

"Beware of practicing your righteousness before other people in order to be seen by them, for then you will have no reward from your Father who is in heaven. "Thus, when you give to the needy, sound no trumpet before you, as the hypocrites do in the synagogues and in the streets, that they may be praised by others. Truly, I say to you, they have received their reward.. ...

Matthew 6:6

But when you pray, go into your room and shut the door and pray to your Father who is in secret. And your Father who sees in secret will reward you.

I recited these versus in class, explained that the significance to me was to show that dressing up all fancy and going to church was not necessary. I could be with God, without going to church…..THAT floated away like a lead balloon. I was told that I needed to take these assignments seriously. My example was quickly dismissed and another topic was chosen. The hardest part were the snickers from others in the class.

If instead, it had been explained to me that the power and energy generated when people get together for a common goal is infinitely more powerful then when you do pray by yourself I would have learned something 25 years earlier than it became apparent to me. The teacher lost the opportunity to explain to me that religion was more than a theology and that it was a way for people to learn to reconnect with not only with their higher selves, but with the higher selves of others, also. In fact, every religion is a "school" designed for those who need to have an easy way to establish a connection to the greater part of themselves and may one day resemble the blue people in the movie Avatar as they sat under the tree generating energy as a group with a common goal.

I had faith in that there was a greater part of me that was still a mystery, however, that part of me did not align with the theology I was taught in school or on Sunday. I began to see that it was not my faith that is in question, but is that theology and methods used by man to communicate faith to others that seems to always fall short or need to be evolved.

This is how that cycle was broken. In my junior year of high school, again a catholic school, I was confronted with an assignment which took me back to my experience in 8th grade. Learning from my previous experience, this time I went to the teacher after class and relayed the same verses and my thoughts on the matter. I realize now I did this in order to see the teacher's reaction and ensure I did not fail the assignment, not to discover what he was about to reveal to me. The teacher listened to me thoughtfully, then said "This sounds like a good argument for your paper and I look forward to reading it." Wow, what a difference and this simple statement caused me to want to understand different theologies and people's view on faith. That teachers simple comments re-evolved my view on the religion and really taught me the concept of learning different perspectives. It took me years to realize that no version of faith is wrong, so all my teachers and friends who ever said to me "You must have faith", they were right, but now I say to them, you must gain a different perspective. What gets people twisted up in knots is the theology, how a person interprets it, and then feeds it to other people. Our spiritual guidance already exists within us....If we have faith, if you can remember.

If people follow your words; their interpretation of what you have said may be twisted or used in a way you never meant for it to be used. You may read this book and determine for yourself that things should be a certain way, however, that is your interpretation of what you are reading, but may not mean what the words are saying. It is only how you are able to interpret them at the time you read them. The answers to faith, love, and growth are within you, once you can hear past the noise of your world and ask yourself the right questions. When your perspective changes, it is likely how you read the words in this book will change and hold a different meaning, also.

In the next paragraph I will use a label to demonstrate to you that I am qualified for what I am about to say. I recognize that I am doing this and I do it consciously, but would you have picked up on it? People do it to you every day and how we are taught to treat the label varies, but the fact that we do this unconsciously is something you may want to change on your road to being a conscious listener. Sooo... Now that I have made you aware of it, you can judge the label consciously.

I am a Reiki Master and have taught several students how to move energy to help reduce stress and promote healing within themselves and others. At least one person in every class has asked me how long it would take to become a Reiki Master. My response is always the same. I look at them and say "You are already a Reiki Master; you just need to listen to yourself and remember. I ask, "How long will it take for you to do that?"

It took me decades to realize that when I listened to myself that, as a human being, I did not need theology to have faith and be spiritual. However, those who used theology to engage their faith were just as perfect as everyone else. They simply needed something different in their lives than I required in mine. You see this is why people need to keep re-evolving religion, some say they lose faith, but I believe faith remains a constant and it is the theology that becomes less meaningful over time as people evolve. You may ask, "If this is true then why do church memberships continue to grow within some sects?" Well examine the purpose of the sect. Those religions still growing are renowned for their community service and service to others. There is a basic human "need" to feel like you have been helpful to others. This need may be selfless, but can also be selfish. I am sure you can refer back to the examples of the stampedes in the church parking lot I put in the book earlier and quickly identify some examples yourself. I know I have a lifetime of them. Today, people use theology as the proverbial shepherd, but that time is changing as people begin to listen to that small voice inside them. This evolution takes time and baby steps. It will take some time understanding being a dark walker. There is no easy transition before the next big step.

Every step in this book is important, but a key transition is happening here. You are beginning to see, in the dark and you are turning the lights up slowly to adjust to the brightness as we go. It is through this step that you begin to see and to "know' what you know. Some may say you have found faith, but don't let that stop you from being excited about it. You may be so invigorated by what you have learned that you are ready to tell the world. I caution you here because not everybody is ready for you to share what you have learned on your journey. They may have a negative reaction, completely dismiss it, or argue with you about it.

Imagine this. You have spent a majority of your life relying on the dark walker to help you avoid the pitfalls and predators of life as you wander through it in the dark. You begin to seek your own light and in the process the dark walker helps you on this journey. At some point you get a glimpse of light and become so excited about what you have learned. You do not completely understand, but feel you have to share it. Guess what. The world around you has not been on that same journey, many are happy to be roaming around in the dark. Some of them have seen the work involved with getting to the light and have purposefully avoided it! So your first thought is to share your excitement with them and blind them with your light. What do you think the response is going to look like?

In a flash the world focuses on consuming your energy because you blinded everybody you talked to. It needs to be enough that you see, others do not want to see what you see. When they do, they will ask you. They will seek out help in making their own journey. This book is for them....For you.

Be mindful that getting a glimpse is not the whole story. If you share too soon you may meet someone who is masterful at turning you around and turning everything you were excited about into coincidence or something that had nothing to do with your own brilliance and light. They will try to dim your light, to bring you back into the fold and if you are not careful you will go there just to avoid being different.

The flaw so many of us make is in the method, not the message. The method we want to follow is "Hey everybody, look what I figured out!! Come here and let me share it with you!" The result is a horde of zombies closing in on you with vampires driving them in your direction. The method is not to go and wake people up or shine a bright light in their eyes, the method is to wait for them to come to you. Be patient.

Consider that you are moving to a place where your energy will flow consistently, the vampires and zombies will come to you. Try and distract you or become curious about you. Remember you took this journey with me to learn how to grow and expand *your* understanding of self. When the time is right those you care most about will present themselves to you, but only when you are ready for them, so keep learning and exposing yourself to more of your own questions.

I find it interesting that people say they do not meditate because they can't be still for that long in their mind. Even this practice is a process; do not flip on the light. Take into account that you can sit and look at a beautiful sunset in silence and peace or stopping on a sunny day to absorb the energy from the sun....That is meditating. The process of just being. You did it for nine months straight when you began this life. No technology, no distractions, just being with you. The noise has disrupted you, made you forget. Coffee on the porch in the early morning with no music or phone is a simple form of meditation. Again there are longer more involved forms of beneficial meditation, but first hear what your heart is singing, then you can look for a more advanced forms of seeing your light.

So where does all of this leave the atheist? Exactly where they want to be. As a dark walker you begin to see that this exposure provides you an enhancement to your own life experience. After all, how can you have a representation of "some-thing" and not have an equal and opposite representation of "no-thing"? The South Park TV show had a segment called "Abandon all Hope" that can be found on the Internet. In this clip all these people were standing in hell and asked the "Hell Director" what religion "got it right" if they were all in hell. The South Park creators picked out the Mormons as the true "chosen people". I always wondered how inspirational it could have been if the chosen people were actually the atheists. I can just see the hell director saying "Guess what everybody; it was the atheists who came closest to the correct answer.

I am not saying the atheist is right or wrong I am saying that they have reached a level of awareness and accepted their physical being as their ultimate limitation. Many people are like this and they all make stellar zombies with the ability to consume day to day activities, but occasionally will awaken to the fact that there may be something else out there... Before they go back to sleep. There is nothing "out there" after death because it is all within us. The atheist does not believe there is a part of them that they cannot see or will not process because it does not live in the physical world and it is just too uncomfortable to move or question outside what the five senses can provide as feedback. I think something everyone can learn from the perspective of the atheist. It is the fact that there is "nothing out there" and it is all inside of us.

Consider that each of us is a part of everything. Imagine that being a part of literally everything all at once, everything that has ever been or ever will be is of course part of the definition of energy and of course science has indisputable proof that our bodies have an energy field that emanates from each of us. So when does this transformation from being a part of everything to being a part of one thing take place? At birth we were separated from everything by the very fact of this energy being shoved into a tiny "being". It would make sense to me that a being of infinite proportions suddenly being separated from all and forced to travel through life "alone" could grow to believe that there is nothing after what the physical form really is. The atheist does nothing in the name of theology, so this in turn holds him closer to the true nature of the Inner child that is the bond to their eternal energy.

This is the energy which energizes our being, follows the laws of physics, spirituality, and every other type of definition for energy and it will "Be".... infinitely. If you can follow this line of thinking then a person, atheist, who believes that there is no higher being; is right. They represent that eternal energy themselves and are a part of what has always been and will always be. It is believed by an atheist that when they die that it is the end, again because this is a material existence that is a very true statement and one that they in their heart know to be true. That when they die their body will cease and the material world they know will end.

It was the atheists who got it right....." Why? Well because they do not believe in anything outside of themselves and the idea of angels and harps and clouds is no more realistic than eternal damnation. I give a lot of credit to the atheist, there is nothing outside yourself that is needed and when this physical life is over, well... it is over. They are right, it is over and for that form there is nothing more to it.

The spark of energy moves off to the next great adventure, so while the atheist may be considered awake, they are only awake to their physical selves because to them that is really all they want to be awake to on this journey. We should be thankful to have the opportunity to experience that enhancement of self. Does this mean I am an atheist? The label holds no more or less value to me than the label of being a Reiki Master, but find the questions about this and judgements associated with the labelling fascinating in my journey. This is just one example of the opportunities that lay before you as a dark walker. When you begin to understand the new questions and enhancements to perspective then you will increase your own awareness.

It is so critical to understand that as your perspective evolves that the universe will evolve to provide you opportunities to use your courage. These opportunities will be brought to you, you will not need to go and find them. Take this as a sign that you are walking in the dark, maneuvering through your experiences and able to just see the outlines of things as your eternal child is slowly turning up the lights, as you experience these new enhancements to your reality.

Ready for some more perspective? A single human existence while expansive and full of experiences will never yield all the possible human experiences, so we must have others share their experiences with us to further enhance our journey. Now remember where we get our competitive nature and knowing this; it is hard for people to not view this in a competitive "right" or "wrong" struggle. Our past society has made us into a labeling and judgmental being , but now as a dark walker, you should be able to start to see these differences in perspective as enhancements to your human experience.

I have never been incarcerated and hopefully never will know the feeling of having my freedom taken from me, but some people have. I have never lost a child and had to experience that grief firsthand, but there are those who have. Imagine the freedom there must be for the atheist, by not believing there is anything greater than the life you currently lead and that all mysteries of the world can be explained by science. All three of these examples are an enhancement to life experiences without having to live those experiences. In this way you can participate in the energies around these experiences of others. It allows you to relate to the experience. Similar to a situation where you allow a mother, who loses a child, to cry on your shoulder and for you to feel empathy for her loss. We have the opportunities in our lives to share these experiences with other people's lives, to enhance our own and provide us with a fuller life's journey, but there is a quick way to kill any enhancement. We can apply our perspective, emotion, and judgment to it rather than allowing it to experience us. We have the potential to carry with us; not only our own experiences, but also any enhancements we experienced through the lives of others. Then we can take all of these experiences and rejoin to the source when our time comes to begin a new journey.

Age and Wisdom

Humanity has aged, but have we gained wisdom through the ages? Sure we have evolved our technology and built a world where we can rely on big corporations for finances, resources, and a rulebook on how to survive in this world. This evolution is obvious as governments create more programs to aid the "under privileged", yet they have no programs to control the over privileged. Why is this? Is this wise as humanity to allow there to be either an upper or lower class? Where is the aged wisdom in this? Wisdom is like a fortune cookie you open it and read inspiring words on a small piece of paper, however, those words when put together are still not knowledge. You do not gain this knowledge until you have dragged them into your experiences. We know humanity has gained knowledge about our external world because we have seen "progress", but we have not felt progress because we have not experienced growth of self as a race of people. As long as we allow this gap to persist we will use external achievements like technology and governments to hide the lack of experiences we have in learning about ourselves.
The truly wise people understand that there are still many zombies and vampires who need the belief in religion to occur for their world to make sense. A wise person does not pull against these activities, but looks for those brief moments where they are asked questions or put in a situation where they can help bring their wisdom for others into a personal experience for both. This is the progress of the enlightened. Sounds easy right?
Here is a situation. I am on vacation with my family in a town in the mountains of Colorado. One day we go to an outdoor craft fair and I am enjoying the beautiful day walking with my wife, 13 year old daughter, who has a friend in tow, and 22 year old daughter, who has her boyfriend in tow. As I walk through the craft fair looking at

the different pieces I come across some beautiful work by a local artist. Soon I realize I am standing with my back to this artist and I feel a pull of energy while she is having a conversation with another person about the arthritis she is having in her hands and how painful it is for her to do her work. My youngest daughter who had been walking with me came and grabbed me by the hand and told me everyone was ready to go. I walked out of the small display area with her. Now what do you do? I was moved to help and bring an experience into the artists reality. By moved, I mean I felt it in my gut and I heard that small voice encourage me to offer assistance. So now courage dictates I go back, introduce myself to this complete stranger in pain and offer some energy work to relieve the pain from her wrists. On the other hand, my family is waiting for me and they want to walk through town, it's close to lunch time, the daughter's boyfriend may be critical of this work that I do and he does not understand it. He may pass judgement if I go back, besides I am on vacation and this is my family time.....All the best reasons I could think to just keep walking, rushed through my head. Then I asked myself what my heart was saying? Was I being courageous about this opportunity? Not so easy now is it? All of these thoughts in less than 30 seconds. I stopped my daughter, told her to go let her mom know I would catch up....She looked me dead in the eye and said, "Dad you're going back to help her, aren't you?" Talk about powerful; I almost fell over.....Wow....I had not realized she was even aware of the woman's struggle. I took that moment with my daughter to tell her to NEVER stop listening to that voice. That the voice will never steer her wrong and always take care of her. My greatest joy that day came from the lesson my daughter taught me about listening to myself. I understood then that to have wisdom does not always require age or come with a diploma on the wall, but can happen in a single experience through anyone. Some of those moments we have to define our lives can come from our children or at the very least from listening to our own eternal child.

It is interesting that we place so much value on the labels we attach to qualifications, credentials, certifications, scholastic achievements, and educational degrees. They all seem to be designed as a comfort mechanism for people to relinquish their accountability and designate someone as "wise". For example, people will go to see a "therapist" to help them with certain life issues. I hear many conversations that start with "my therapist said..." It is great to have someone who you can bounce ideas off of or share your experiences; until you start using that person as the reason that you are doing the things in your life that you are doing. When you go to see a professional the first thing most people do is look for qualifications. A big diploma on the wall or recommendation from other professionals are ways for a person to become more comfortable with the qualifications of a professional and be willing to pay them for their time. These are all questions of qualification and how a person may be qualified to give you advice allowing you the opportunity to turn over accountability to them because of a piece of paper on the wall.

I always found this practice ironic for both the person seeking the qualification and for the person who required a "qualified" person. To me the irony was in the process, a person who was qualified usually had several years of schooling, but the schooling was an average of four years behind the profession. Now you may say this is not true for all professions, however, what is true is that your eternal child knows more than you could hope to learn in a lifetime and when you are connected, you always have an expert with you. Schooling and papers not required.

Before there was a time when you needed certifications, there were experts with a great "bedside manner". Now we have more certified experts, but their attitude is the pits. Is there a correlation between the educational requirements and the attitudes people have toward the work they do?

I knew several experts who refused to spend the money on certifications in their field because they knew more about the technology than could be put in a test, however, society demanded the qualifications and certifications to prove that a person knew what they were talking about before being hired for a position. I have a car mechanic who I always take my car to get it serviced. He is very personable, does a good job, keeps the car running, and is able to tell me anything and everything about my vehicle, but struggles every time he is forced to go and take a test to update his certification. By struggles I mean he is a real bear and I am surprised his wife has not moved him out to the garage during these testing exercises. I doubt there are many people who know more about my vehicle then he does, however, he takes it very personally when he has to go and certify that he knows what he knows. I can see a correlation between the joy someone has in what they do and the amount of "required" testing that must occur to remain qualified. Move this to an internal level and on a personal level we have the opposite problem, we get very frustrated with that part of ourselves that we do not know. So, to find a way to better understand that part of ourselves we seek out those who are "qualified" to show us the way to find ourselves. WHAT! Really? This type of exercise can take years of therapy only to find out that we already know the way to ourselves, we just have to find a way to remain courageous while experiencing it. For that many times we need a mentor or guide to support us on our journey, remember support, not drive. The greatest qualifications do not come from having a piece of paper that you have spent years achieving or tens of thousands of dollars to educate yourself and a certain field. The greatest qualifications as dark walkers come from our ability to hear other people's eternal child calling out and to be able to provide that critical question at the right time. Over time we lost sight of this and allowed ourselves to be told the way things needed to be, rather than listening to ourselves and believing we were qualified to understand our own energy and existence. After all it is easier to be able to blame somebody else, who is an expert, for things when they go wrong. And while this may be right logically, it is not accurate and now you can feel that too.

Consider that the government provides state run schools for our children. These schools have the curriculum designed for compliance. There is one right answer always presented one way and if you want to get a good grade in a class the most important thing is not the facts, but is if you know what it is the teacher is looking for. In the movie "The Dead Poet's Society", Robin Williams was acting out the part of a teacher who invited his class to open their eyes and see. In the end it was the institution which won the battle, but Robin Williams character was profound enough in a short period of time to ensure the institution did not win the war.

Hopefully, you were graced with one such teacher in your life. This does not need to be a formal teacher in school, but it is someone who invited you to open your eyes, stand on your desk and see the world from a different perspective. Someone did, that is why you are here.

Our parents and our parents' parents have built industry, watched man land on the moon, cured disease and have used technology to destroy human life in the name of preserving it. So now we are in the time of the technology man. Children go to school with cell phones and speak a language in an abbreviated alphabet still curious to most adults. They walk around with music blaring in their ears all hours of the day, not just after school or in the evening, but have the ability to be connected to technology every hour of every day. Previous generations build technology to aid humanity and some of its laborers, but current technology is aiding man in forgetting the accountability that they have for their own eternal child.

The Technology Man

So wait....I know, we are moving into another section of the book and there is a question that has not been answered. How long do you need to be a dark walker? So, here is my question to you, "How long will it take for you to consistently listen to yourself?" I find myself going back to the dark walker state at different points in my life where I can learn more. I evolve, have new challenges and new experiences which bring me to this great place, again. Most of the time when I find myself reverting to being a dark walker it is because of a single element. It is because I miss the darkness. I do not want to be in the space of being aware or helpful to others. It is my darkness I want to appreciate and in that darkness I can find the technology man.

I can give you some level of comfort in knowing that once you're here....Once you have established yourself in the space of a dark walker, you have to want to go back to being a zombie. You have to want to put yourself back in that state.

This section is for those people who were born within the last three decades and have seen advances made by man through the use of technology and began to use it to aid man. Technology then became man's crutch because of its speed to the solutions the technology could create. Man could process material things faster than they could purchase them, and purchase them faster than man could evolve to understand them. Think about how fast the computer industry has changed in the last 10 years and how many computers you have had. The external world is easy to master through the use of technology and that is what man has set out to master momentarily forgetting that they have yet to master themselves.

The Native American Indians were much further along at mastering themselves than the Europeans when they landed on the shores on the Americas. In this era man used technology to take what they wanted because they had been evolving their physical consumption of "things", not their internal self. This cycle has not changed in over 200 years. Several cultures have had a great heritage and were on their way to mastering harmony with the world when technology got in front of that progress and we are continually repeating the mistake to this day by allowing ourselves to get in our own way. Once man used technology as a support to improve life, now technology has been used instead as a model for society. I still have great faith in humanity and believe we are approaching critical mass and a time where technology will stop appealing to man as much, we will become bored with it and look for the next great adventure. For those awake today, they realize, as you do, that the next great adventure beyond technology is an internal journey. Of course there will be those who remain a "technology man" who have no interest in mastering themself, rather interests will remain in the distraction of mastering the world, not harmonizing with it.

Here is the question, what is the true nature of humanity? Which nature of man is operating out of fear? You see no matter how hard we try the one thing we cannot get away from is our own humanity and so long as we remain fearful of ourselves we will be distracted by technology, by competition, by fear of the unknown, and by ego. Many will continue to walk down a path that is unfulfilling, but have really cool gadgets to keep them all distracted. Are you distracted? Have you missed my points in the last several paragraphs because I used the label of "man" rather than Person or human? If so, you have questions you need to address within yourself about how emotionally attached you have become to labels. Yes, again I did it on purpose to make a point. Noise is everywhere, do not let it distract you, do not tie emotion to it!

Man today can use technology for such amazing things and humanity stands in awe of some of these great achievements. Technology allows us to heal faster, identify disease quicker, and travel farther. Yet when man looks inside himself he does not stand in awe of this achievement as he does with technology of his external world. In many ways man still sees infancy and disharmony rather than the wonder and amazement. Why is this? You are brilliant!

If we can agree that at this point in our journey together that our societies define a life based on its physical desires, materials, and experiences, then I think we are getting close to discovering why our eternal child is ignored. If we expand this to include the many times those desires are influenced by mass media noise, and technology distractions, I think we are closer. So now you are here....What is the next question? Maybe feeling a little overwhelmed? Like the deck is stacked against you. So many challenges, so many battles, so much to fight......NOT AT ALL. There is no fight. No battle. No war. Only re- evolving. We live in a great time and so all of these things mentioned are not to be challenged, but to be experienced and enabled as an enhancement to your own experience.

In Star wars "The Empire Strikes Back" Luke Skywalker comes face to face with his arch enemy, Darth Vader, only to find out after the fight that his opponent was really himself. His teacher told him before he went to the swamp for this lesson that he would not need his weapons, but he took them anyway. I can tell you three things as you head off to battle yourself....First, do not view this as a "battle", second all you need is unconditional love, and third, like Luke Skywalker, if you take a weapon with you....You will most assuredly need it.

If now every single theology is right and our ability to experience life is assisted through the enhancement of the beliefs in other people's lives, then on that day we all realize that everyone is right, based on a perspective we have allowed to become a part of our experience. We will be able to use technology to aid us getting there, but we cannot rely on technology to tell us what is inside us that we already know. This process is not about learning, this process is about remembering. You already know all of this, but with technology getting in front of us, we can rely on it to distract us from those answers.

As I type this there are two TV's on in our house. The two programs bleed over each other and are a major distraction to me. This distraction has stopped me; however, I will use technology to put headphones on and listen to some soothing music to get back on course. My point. Technology is not good or evil. However, when we choose to assign things with labels, right or wrong, black or white, then there are issues with the process of connecting to the eternal child and past the dark walker. Staying with the dark walker allows us a path to slipping back into the world of the vampire, where a fight must be fought and a judgment must be passed. It is at these points that you will find yourself in the dark and you WILL stub your toe, trip over the dog, or walk into the door on your way to remembering what it is you already know.

Big corporations are designed to feed the zombie mentality. Go to work 9-5 consuming resources to create more resources to be consumed. The company consumes the zombies who walk through their day to day life doing something they do not enjoy. The big businesses and governments of the world have tipped the scales on greed, lost the balance with those they once controlled through technology and I can see this as a positive change for the journey ahead of us.

On the playground if a child falls the child next to them reaches to help them instinctively and if the child is crying there are times where both children will cry because the one feels the others pain. As adults we see someone carrying a gas can or broken down on the road and we think "That sucks, I hate it when that happens to me." Then the decision, to listen to that internal voice asking that you reach out and help them or is it so noisy in your head that you keep going because there are places to be and people to see? The dark walker and the eternal child are two sides of the same coin. One side is light and the other dark. The technology man can be used to achieve great things on either side of that coin. We cannot escape one or the other based on how humanity has grown. Many of us practice being both through technology. We love the technology and having the ability to communicate with people all around the world, travel by air to see them, or talk on a thin electronic pad with them. The eternal child is a secret that man has forgotten he was the benefactor of and this fact has remained buried for decades within each of us. This secret man has gotten on without for generations so how can it be important. Well it is my point that man has gone as far as they can go in manipulating the exterior world using the framework of technology. People are starting to lose interest in consuming their exterior world and now are beginning to focus on their eternal child.

What is it that the technology man then hopes to accomplish? Love is the answer. Technology was created by man, to aid man, but like other elements of our emotional and physical world it can easily get twisted into a form of love for the gadgets and the material things that create the noise, the noise that causes us not to hear ourselves. This is not technologies fault, this is our choice, but I think the issue is we are doing it without conscious thought. A new version of a phone comes out and everyone stands in line for hours. Why? Not everyone's phone is broken. The technology man has just gone from being an aid to humanity, to being the noise and distraction when this happens.

With the help of failing financial sectors and governments we are all evolving to the point of being awake. Many are angry at the governments and institutions that are failing, taking jobs, and causing economies to destabilize, but is it anger or fear? Fear at having to answer those questions we could avoid for past generations and most of our lives.

There are those who are using mass media to effect change in people both to awaken and to keep them asleep. An example of mass media that swirls in fear is the evening news on most TV stations. They have a political platform they support and they present the news in a certain way. This does nothing to enhance your awakened state, so you must realize you are allowing that negative barrage of media to cause you to fear. This is not to say all mass media is bad, in fact, it can be used to have the opposite effect as well.   A good example of this is someone who has inspired millions of people and was herself inspired by mass media. She began her career as a talk show host "back in the day" when there were a lot of daytime talk show hosts. She was one of many who were competing for ratings and battling it out to get on top. If it was possible to go back and watch the broadcasts done by Oprah Winfrey in her earliest days you would see that there were many times that she moved through the motions and was "zombie like". This was standard among the other daytime talk show hosts too; all pursuing ratings, and doing shows the producers wanted to have done to enhance the ratings. There were those rare shows where you could see Oprah's true passion come out and her awakening began as she was energized by the topics and people she would interview, her questions became connected to the person she was interviewing, and she started to find her bliss. For many years, though, more often than not it was ratings based. Then tragedy struck the talk show industry. A violent crime brought the entire talk show industry to the verge of extinction and shows began getting pulled off the air. Some shows re-evolved and were saved like Oprah's show who seemed to find a niche' in the "human interest" stories. Today, she is extremely popular and produces shows based on feeding the soul not the ratings. This is an example of mass media being used to aid humanity. What has inspired her, her success, and the service she has provided to others, have all brought her to her bliss. The amazing thing is that when you examine true success stories, somewhere in the story there is tragedy.   Something had to happen for those involved to awaken themselves, then once awake, the person had to desire to stay awake and boldly go on a journey inside themselves.......To find their eternal child.

TO BOLDLY GO

I grew up in what my father affectionately nicknamed the "boob-tube" era, called this because he believes television produced a lot of….well….boobs. I admit I spent a lot of time watching television as a child, because I was sure that if there was nothing of value, it certainly would not be aired on TV. This led me to believe that the movies produced and TV shows aired must all be like Star Trek, each with subtle messages to us that we must look for throughout the show.

On September 8, 1966, NBC aired Gene Rodenberry's science fiction TV show Star Trek. A science fiction show illustrating the powers of technology and the ability for the human race to "boldly go where no man has gone before." Oddly, for every new species encountered, for every new planet they beamed down to, the issues and challenges of the 1970's were disguised in the TV show characters, planets, and costumes found around the universe. If you are a conscious observer or a child you can see this. The difference in the new Star Trek movies, while very entertaining, full of action and incredible special effects, there is no underlying message for the active observer to feed on during these movies. They are simply entertainment where you are led from beginning to logical conclusion.

When I was younger I would watch a movie or show consciously and look for clues from the actors of how the plot would develop. I did not rely on the producer to take me by the hand and lead me blindly down the path of entertainment. I could do this with almost any movie and when I perfected this process and put it into practice it drove my friends and family crazy because I could name the killer, identify the bad guy, or spot the traitor before the plot revealed it. I really thought this was the goal of movies at the time. To find the underlying message or discover the plot before it was revealed. I carried this forward into my life and started watching peoples actions and found a way to place a higher value on their actions and paid little credence to the words coming out of their mouth if their actions were not aligned.

This is the next step for you in this book. To find that place inside of you that speaks to you about what it is you are observing. If all the world is a stage and you are an actor, then it is time to see if the producers can outwit you, so I would actively observe the shows and come up with the answers before the show reveals it. What is the value of seeing things clearly? To see these things you must let go of old prejudices, thoughts and feelings. The value to you is your ability to know, not only hear the voice, but can act on it from a place of unconditional love. So now that you have found your voice and have courage to use it, now you must boldly go and start looking at those things you are allowing to entertain you and take up your time.....This will in turn allow you the opportunity to let go of previous perceptions and beliefs. This will require courage, integrity, and yes probably some stumbling in the dark, but on the other side of this discovery process are some freedoms you did not know you had. One of these discoveries will be your ability to become the observer, without contributing negative energy around a topic. The ability to attach yourself to things through love, not anger, giving you the ability to see each side of an issue with utmost clarity.

Think about your current path with this book. You are consuming the words in this book, maybe you are skipping paragraphs or chapters, maybe you are mad as hell at me for bringing things into question that have always been foundational for you, or maybe you have found something of value in the words I have placed on these pages. This energy is an enhancement to our self and it can be said that these enhancements are the song of the soul, others may say these are the events we need to become aware of before we can "follow our heart".

The heart is an organ, a physical manifestation that feeds the physical form, right? But we cannot physically see it unless we cut the body open, however, somehow we have faith it is there....In every human being.....It has to be there, right? A blood pump station, is that all it is? The brain controls the thought process and is the central control for all information being processed. The heart is simply there to supply blood to all the organs including the brain. What about the studies done at the Heart Math Institute showing that it is actually the heart that is feeding the brain the information it needs? We spend a lot of money trying to discover how we unlock the full potential of the brain. What if using 100% of our brains capacity required we unlock that potential by unlocking the hearts potential first? How does that feel to you? The heart leads the brain, not the other way around. In order to use more of the brains potential you must first understand the hearts potential. To do this you must first go into a place that mankind has been avoiding for as long as we have walked this tiny planet. If these two physical organs were to grow and the capacities realized; then how would they understand the third part of self? Yes the third member of the

trinity, the eternal child, soul, higher self, use whatever word feels good here. The father, the son, and the Holy Ghost make up the Roman Catholic theology, but the parallels to me seem uncanny and too coincidental. So line these up….
The father…..The scientist…..The brain.
The son…..sent to teach unconditional love……The heart…..
The Holy Spirit……the eternal child….our higher self

Let's lighten this up and have some fun with this now that we can play the conscious observer and see within ourselves. What happens when we look at the underlying message for a classic like "The Wizard of Oz"? A child's search for a brain, heart, and soul was manifested through three beloved characters. Now, I believe the reason the cowardly lion was not searching for his soul was because in that day and age if he was searching for his soul; the formidable theological institutions would have hung this movie out to dry. So courage was an acceptable trait to replace the soul and again a cornerstone trait needed for any transformation, so it is an excellent substitute for the soul.
In the Wizard of Oz we are introduced to a young girl faced with obstacles and evils on her journey through life. It starts as the youth angers that her black and white world would turn on her and her little dog, that the institutions were going to take something from her that she loved and her first reaction was to run away. She tries to run from her problems, but discovers this creates a "whirlwind" of bigger issues. She finds herself swept away from her reality by a force of nature into a land of vibrant color and fanciful characters. The story starts from the adults perspective of black and white, the way of the world…..But a child's view is not black and white, as they start their journey through this life with rose colored glasses.
Dorothy arrives in Oz to find a colorful land filled with amazing people and a world just like she imagined it should be? Well as soon as she got there, she wanted to return home. I guarantee the first time you "boldly go" you will want to go back to the safety of what is known and expected of you.
So Dorothy is off to see the Wizard and along the way she finds the physical representations of the heart, the brain, and courage. They travel this road together and are challenged by none other than the evil vampire... huh witch. Who wants something she cannot have and is not hers to consume. She threatens the entire group and stalks them all the way to OZ. They have been told that in OZ there is a great and powerful wizard who can get them what they seek. In

the end, they find that OZ is a magical place filled with horses that change color and people who all have an established society of peace and harmony. This harmony and peace changes when the society is threatened by the witch and Dorothy and company are sent on a mission. Do not think this is not going to happen to you, if you decide to boldly go on this mission. You might even say the zombies kicked Dorothy and company out because they became afraid.

Then at the end of the story you discover that the wizard is simply a man that has learned to use technology and maybe as much as 11% of his brain. This man has trinkets for each character who feels at a loss, so a diploma, a medal, and a heart shaped clock. Each of these items representing the story of this young girls search for the trinity of herself, which in the end turns out that it really is all right inside her. A timeless classic. And you know why? Because while the film was released in 1939 we can all still relate to the journey of self and that message just below the surface. Evolution? This journey is still something we all continue to search for. We already know this. We have simply forgotten it, but it has been captured in this movie.

As you Courageously go on your journey for your heart and mind you may find yourself getting in the way. Your brain will try and get in the way with logic, but if you keep pressing on you will hear the divine spark and what you will finally discover....Is that you knew all of this, all along.

To understand that we all carry a divine spark, that we are all made up of the same stuff, and that intellectually, given a scale of 1 to 100% brain capacity .....we are all nit wits because we have ignored our heart!

Instead we need to bring things into physical reality so it has to be something we can hang on a wall, pin to our chest, or carry in our pocket. Then and only then can we feel qualified to further separate ourselves from each other when really we should be headed in the opposite direction. The true hidden genius behind this story is Dorothy climbing into the balloon and "leaving" all of these physical representations of found treasures behind to move back into her space of intention, back to her farm in Kansas as she awakens in her black and white reality. In this reality she shows gratitude and love for all those intangible things she has and appreciates. The producer was sure to bring those actors into the black and white reality to show that these are three things were with her all along and that they were always with her. Interesting? If you are awake this is what you see. You see the story in the story, the life behind the veil of humanity. And yes to boldly go is scary as hell, like riding a tornado, or a bicycle down a steep hill; however, when you wake up you will see things very clearly.

Technology

You are not a zombie if you have been reading this far into this book....Zombies rely on consuming information through mass media and technology offering immediate gratification without needing to apply much thought to it. A book like this is too individualized and separate for them to bother with unless they are either forced to read it....or found a cliff notes audio version they can listen to. I love technology. It has produced some of man's greatest achievements, but also some of the loudest noise when trying to hear the eternal child in you. I have spent the majority of my adult life earning a living through understanding how technology works. I consulted with big companies, directed and managed technology teams and projects, and even taught some very technical classes to some very smart people. I like all the latest gadgets including game consoles, smart phones, and I understand that technology is one of the greatest weaknesses I have when approaching how I spend my time. My life experiences have shown me that I am marketable in the area of technology, can get a good paying job, support my family, and live a comfortable life with all the bells and whistles I want. When I stopped the noise and started listening to what it was I wanted, really wanted, I found that working in the area of technology was what society had prepared me to do, but was not what my soul wanted me to do. It simply was not of service to anyone, except the technology.

The original premise for the creation of technology was to help aid man in further developing an understanding themselves, however, technology has taken on a life of its own and rather than being an aide it has become a society unto itself. We have not lost the ability to understand this and as you go through the steps in this process one thing you will begin to understand is the requirement to unplug yourself. Now, I am not asking you to get rid of your TVs or disconnect your Internet access, but to establish a place and time for these activities will help reduce the noise level so you can hear yourself.

Many of us wake in the morning to the sound of an alarm clock either music or news. I try very hard to ensure I am not listening to news about the day, first thing in the morning. It is hard to establish a good frame of mind for yourself when the first thing you hear when you wake up is bad news. Instead I walk through the house thinking two thoughts. The first is "Harmony for my day". This prepares me to understand that my day will occur in perfect harmony (even the bad stuff will happen as planned). My second thought is gratitude. Gratitude for my ability to walk around the kitchen, just the simple act of using my five senses to navigate through my morning routine. Harmony and Gratitude win out over any source of music or morning newscast. Many people prepare breakfast and turn the TV on or turn on a radio to stay connected or establish a connection to their world for the day. I feel empathy for those people who are preparing breakfast in the morning and are already on the phone with their job while the news is blaring in the background. It is amazing how many people show up at work and the topic of conversation revolve around news media events. I think the most disturbing example of technology gone awry is walking into a public men's bathroom , hearing a phone ring, and hearing a voice from one of the stalls say "hello". There are times and places for technology to aid us in our journey to better understand ourselves and each other. I cannot think of a better tool for our children than the Internet when used to understand and relate ourselves to other cultures. This technology we call the Internet has provided great opportunities for humanity to re-evolve, but has also offered humanity the opportunity to slide backwards as well.

Unfortunately, a byproduct of technology has been a desire for instant gratification. This is not new and has not been created by technology, but has been an enhancement as a result of the speed at which technology changes our society. As a result people will have a desire to hurry the process and seek instant gratification. Remember people both young and old, have been conditioned by technology and convinced the world is a certain way because someone, somewhere, has said it was so. It may have been a TV personality, radio personality, family member, or coworker, but what was said has been consumed. Now imagine the rate of consumption that can occur with a technology like the Internet. Compared to 20 years ago consumption of information through technology is like drinking water from a fire hose! I know I can't keep up with my daughters Facebook posts, likes, status updates, and polls!

I stated in the opening paragraph of this section that you are not a zombie because you have made it this far in the book , but there is a question to ask yourself. Can the work you do make you a zombie?

124

Absolutely! If you do something you have no passion for, get up every day to do the same thing, and have no spark for doing it, you are a zombie in step two and just faking it. So if what you do, is not who you are, you need the courage to boldly bridge that gap. One of the most interesting groups I have encountered on the Internet, trying to bridge that gap, is the group known as Anonymous. This group has found a way to have its voice heard through the use of technology and bridge the gap between the use of that technology and the abuses being manifested by the technology. This activist group, also called hacktivist's, have found a way to use the Internet to have their voices heard. This is a good place for a dark walker to begin their journey in realizing the difference between what they hear about this group through mass media and what activities this group is involved with. Any group openly attacked by media and politics to instill fear gets me asking questions. So, when I first started researching this group I quickly discovered the website used by many of them to post information and pictures. Many of the pictures, by today's social standards of acceptance, were shocking and made me feel uncomfortable. Then to change the perspective I realized that this is the point of those pictures. This culture did not care about social acceptance and interestingly it was the society that created the culture. To bring you outside the box of society and help you realize that what you are being told may not actually be the way the world is perceived by you. As with any group, there are extremists, however the charter of this group is to help those who cannot help themselves through the use of technology. Rarely has there been a group of members who are all members working towards a common goal without an established leadership. This group has affected the world order and impacted a region of the world enough to assist with the resignation of a world leader. If you view any group and the impact that group has had on society you may find, through your own research, that this group stands above many of the established groups out there today. The problem with this group is that it does fly in the face of the established institutions and society itself. It is acting as that bright light in the middle of the night. The fear created by this group causes the institution to fear, the zombies to wake up and freak out. This worries the powerful vampires of the world who are trying to maintain the balance.

The folks in this group are acting as individuals with a common belief, they execute that belief based on a majority belief without leadership, using technology as an aid in their efforts, and are creating world change without requiring they be paid back in any way. This is a group of individuals who have used technology to create independent thought about specific areas and the beauty of the thought is that others will weigh in on this thought as well. Some of the responses and feedback may be less than flattering and could be called brutally honest, but it is independent just the same. So when this group of like-minded individuals gets together and determines that something needs to change they use technology to help aid in that change. The way they use the technology is not in line with socially accepted methods in some cases, however, it is effective and the group stands as an example of our need to re-evolve not only the institutions we currently use, but the way we look at the use of the technology we have enslaved ourselves to. Understand one other thing about the creation of any subculture. Society creates it by revolving itself. When both parents went back to work to make ends meet, when kids started going home to an empty house, when technology and internet access became a method to entertain......What subcultures are our society creating today through our current activities?

Money

"Money makes the world go round" this saying is in the hearts and minds of both zombies and vampires everywhere. In fact, if you want to see the true nature of the zombies and vampires surface, remove the concept of money as being a stabilizing force in the "evolved humanity". Many cannot imagine a world that is not governed by some form of currency. Words like apocalypse and doomsday are heard from many people. Money is one of the most powerful wheels in our experience today. A wheel is something that keeps us moving, not unlike a hamster on his wheel. He can really move on the wheel, but no matter how fast that wheels spins the hamster still goes nowhere. Money is a wheel of security for society and is something we spend a great deal of time instilling in our children. This wheel is designed to provide man a financial certainty in his life. This certainty allows man to run and receive something he can later trade for other resources which he will consume in one manner or another. What other wheels have we created? What hamster wheels do you run in place on?

When I was 16 years old I had been given the family car. I was told I needed to maintain the car and pay for the gas if I wanted to go anywhere. This extended to responsibilities for car insurance and the need for money. Now that I had the ability to go out with friends I needed a way to pay for my car and my fun, so I got a job. From that point on money became a driving force in everything I did because of the money wheel. The better the job the nicer the car or house. This was my experience and is what I saw not only within my own family, but within those families around me. It was not until after I left the military and began thinking about what it was I wanted to do that I realized I was basing my future on money. I was looking at jobs and careers based on how much income I could make in a year. It was at this point that I added an additional criteria to this process I wanted to enjoy making money. I wanted to ensure what I did was something I truly enjoyed. So while I am still running on the wheel governed by money at least I had the opportunity to pick the wheel and realized for myself that it was in fact a continuous process I would have to adjust for while money was a driving factor for humanity.

I failed. Miserably! If you have ever watched a hamster on his little wheel you will occasionally see him trip or the wheel gets ahead of him and he ends up getting spun around by the force of the wheel and dumped off. This was me. I spent a good deal of time doing something I enjoyed, that made me a good living, but the only time I was really happy was when I was doing something that was making me no money.

Coaching people and having the opportunity to share what I know about Reiki are experiences I cherish and always look forward to, but in the midst of all this I had to live a "double" life and created a lifestyle that required I run on a different wheel. The funny thing is every person gets to pick their own hamster wheel. Recently I discovered that what I am and what I do need to align, so I have jumped off of the wheel and am scared to death of what is going to happen in the years to come.

The saying goes "Every man has his price." For many this price is related to the materials of our world. This may be a car, a house, maybe even a mate. So it is this wheel which they set in motion for them, by them, and ultimately is controlled by their actions and then manifested through their thoughts. They create their world around the material gain for....what? The cause for using this wheel could be noble, for self-interests, starving orphans, or loved ones. Maybe the goal is less noble and monetary gain is related to fancy cars and gold chains. Again as with technology, money can be a great aid to people as long as it does not become a society unto itself and should not dictate your way of life by trading something you are passionate about doing, for something that gets you a nice house.

This brings some serious questions to the surface for you and the eternal child to wrestle through.

At 16, I was not handed the keys to a truck load of money and told to follow my dreams. At 16 if I did not need to have money, to support my car habit, it is likely that I would not have gotten a job; but society is set up so that you can start to contribute to your society at age 16 and now in the USA is designed to ensure you continue to contribute until you are 65.

When you start to contribute you discover the first step in the process includes competition. When you interview for a job it is likely that there's more than one person trying to get the job, the reward for winning is a paycheck, but there comes a point where the paycheck is not enough. When this price is self-realized it may become something viewed by the individual as regret. The advantage to having money is that there are many vices obtainable with enough money to drown out the regret. These regrets have been around for centuries...Scoff if you want, but the betrayal of Jesus was for money by a trusted friend who believed 30 pieces of silver would be enough to drown out the regret. The presidential election in the United states is competed for every four years by those who have the financial ability to compete, not by the best statesmen available to its people. This gives every American over the age of 18 the ability to regret the past four years, be emotional about it through the election process and pick another person who has been bought into the system. We have gained wisdom as humanity, but we are doing it very slowly. To date not enough of us have brought this into our personal experience to have evolved past the need for the money wheel. Money was a wheel humanity was racing on and is still racing on to this day.

I do not believe the goal is to eliminate the idea or need for the monetary system's, however, the monetary system's should be understood as noise that will disconnect you from that voice inside of you. Money, technology, politics, governments, all of these wheels were originally put in place to aid humanity, now they drive humanity. The idea is not to dismantle these aids, but to help people to awaken to the fact that these are aids and not masters of our life.

Relationships

A very poor man lived with his wife. One day, his wife, who had very long hair asked him to buy her a comb for her hair to grow well and to be well-groomed. The man felt very sorry and said no. He explained that he did not even have enough money to fix the strap of his watch he had just broken. She did not insist on her request. The man went to work and passed by a watch shop, sold his damaged watch at a low price and went to buy a comb for his wife. He came home in the evening with the comb in his hand ready to give to his wife. He was surprised when he saw his wife with a very short haircut. She had sold her hair and was holding a new watch band. Tears flowed simultaneously from their eyes, not for the futility of their actions, but for the reciprocity of their love.

What does this story mean to you? Again consider that the story is based on the principles of wisdom, but if you have NEVER been truly poor can you still relate to sacrifices described in this story? What if you have been married several times, none of them resulting in pleasant feelings. Can you relate to the story and what perceptions would you carry from it? Love? Love that is greater than self?

What causes a vampire to wake up? In every vampire story I have seen it has always been the power of love. The essence of this power breaks down to the most powerful energy we can understand in our current human form. The power of this energy can tie us up in knots and launch us into orbit "in a heartbeat". This is the same energy the vampire will skillfully drain from others, but still cannot quench the thirst for another person's energy.

Take a moment, you already know this answer....You see what is coming next don't you! Isn't it great!! The vampire and zombies look for love externally to themselves. They have not awakened to the fact that the love they are seeking is an unconditional love they must first have for themselves. You got it! Now contemplate this as a conscious observer.....What areas of your life do you see people draining the energy from each other because they have yet to look inside themselves? So we get to the basis of this book. It is the evolution of the life sucking forces around us today. Why are you so tired at the end of the workday? Who drained you today? Relationships with others and experiences we've had ourselves cause us to perceive this type of wisdom in several different ways. A relationship is a word on a piece of paper until it is put into practice. The word "relationship" will cause some people to cringe and others to think of their significant other, or a dear friend. The relationship we will refer to in this section will refer to none of these outside entities. The relationship that must be considered in this section is the relationship you have with yourself. To boldly go into that space that has been carrying so much "baggage" from the past takes a lot of courage. The weight that we carry around and subject ourselves to, based on our past; needs to be addressed for us to be able to move forward.

To be loved by someone external is something special, but to not love yourself will impact your ability to reciprocate that love.

Humanity is the only creature that creates opportunities for an enlightened future, but has chosen to live in a world of regret based on things that have happened in the past. The past events cannot be changed, so we do the next best thing, we distract ourselves with regret. We try to resolve the world issues, by actively trying to change society and the institutions that run the cultures of the world today. Imagine this…..If we evolve ourselves, teach our children, mentor those who cross our path, and deal with our own baggage, would the institutions and societies of the world not self-correct? Would we need regret any longer to distract us?

Isn't this why you have read this book? To rid the world of zombies and vampires. This is a daunting task, but to help the world you must first vanquish your zombie and your vampire. Saying you are dedicated to fixing the world is easy, a distraction, but who is going to enlighten you? You must be able to hear the eternal child, then have the courage to follow that voice while consciously observing and being observed by the world.

By being involved as a mentor or teacher when the opportunities present themselves to you; you are causing a peaceful shift and re-evolution of humanity by being here. By walking in the dark and slowly turning the lights up, by boldly stepping forward into the areas of greater brightness and dealing with those things you find within yourself with courage and passion.

Find a way to become comfortable within your own skin, and love the experience and journey of being you. By forgiving yourself of regret and energy offensives done to you it leaves room for you to love. Doing this you will enhance your own "hearing" and your ability to use the wisdom inside you that you have not been able to hear for so long.

Now, when you decide to step boldly into this place you may have never gone here before….. it may feel like a great weight has been lifted, as you begin dealing with your baggage. There is another feeling as well, you will need to deal with this feeling head on or you will repeat this entire process. This process caused me to bump around in the dark for years.

Let's use the analogy of a bucket of water. In this bucket you have been carrying around these negative energies for a very long time.

In that time you have adjusted to the weight of the bucket and it now feel like a part of you. You do not even really notice the weight anymore unless you focus on it. One day you decide to empty the bucket. You feel lighter because the weight is gone and now you can be "free" of that energy. The thing is you have gotten so used to having something there now that it is empty you feel off balance. It may feel like an empty hole or a part of you has been lost. Don't worry what has been lost is the anger, frustration, or other negative emotions you have been feeding off of have been released, creating this imbalance or "hole". Soon it becomes frustrating because now you do not have that negativity to feed on......Believe me I know this is a scary feeling.

To be at that place where you release the need for those emotions and can replace it with unconditional love is an amazing feeling, but is a lot of work. This work starts with you re-evolving that relationship with yourself, deciding you will make that connection with yourself, and trust yourself to boldly and courageously follow your heart and experience your bliss. To get there, it all starts with forgiveness. The forgiveness of self!

FORGIVENESS

For generations, humanity has wrapped its significance in the domination of our external world. We have spent thousands of years learning to dominate each other, our resources, our planet, even our technology, and now we must learn to face ourselves. We have managed to place technology in front of that fact and to use it as a distraction to keep us entertained, however, many people are seeing through this distraction and waking up their relationship with self. They now realize the time wasted, the lessons lost, and those missed opportunities to teach their children something they are just now learning. Here at this moment, as you read these pages and allow the words to be absorbed into your conscious thought, absorb this as well. All of this is perfect. The timing is exactly as it should be, you reading this book is timed exactly when it should be read. The lessons both learned and missed happened as they should have. It is all perfect and regretting the past has no room in your brilliant and full future.

Generations of humanity have come and gone. Each sharing the commonality of being in human form, the heart of man all beats from the same place in the chest, we each bleed the same and require the same type of oxygen to sustain the life in our physical form, this cannot be disputed by anyone on this tiny planet. Still knowing these facts have not been enough for any generation to really realize it is more than the physical form that drives our experiences. Man continues to make himself his own worst enemy by segregating self from each other on a physical level and separating ourselves from our own eternal child who is begging us to do one thing. Forgive. This lack of comprehension makes man a brilliant creator and sophisticated destroyer, both the man and the child, the heaven and the hell, the alpha and the omega.

We are motivated by two things, our history and the future, yet only one we can influence. Man is destined to remain in this existence as long as he cannot forgive those things he can no longer influence. History cannot be changed only manipulated so that it may be fed on by future generations. For us to move on we must recognize that our history is like a memory. We remember things through our own eyes, we see things from our own perspective and so we label that as a "fact". Yet there are other perspectives, other views which are also "facts". Remember the ability to have multiple profound truths and that man has been fighting over historical facts for thousands of years based on one perspective and felt by one emotion. Fear. This is not the fear of being wrong or ego, this is a fear of setting these childish differences of history aside and actually examining who we are on the inside. We fear what we cannot dominate, label, or control when we are looking at the physical nature of our existence. Now the eternal child inside of us is the part of us that wants us to move past the history of hate and negative emotion to a place where we can all celebrate our magnificent being in a place of unconditional love. Those that thrive on fear are unawake, so instead of listening to that inner self they treat history as a memory, our present as perspective, and our future as something to fear. Is it any wonder so many people have decided to remain unawake? It is easier.

Man is a strange creature. We have this word….regret. Not only can we use this word to punish ourselves for things we did in the past, but we can use this word to punish ourselves for things we failed to do in our past. Or things done to our parents…..Or their parents……WOW! This is another whole class of regret that is related to generation regret. This regret has been taught to you by those who have suffered in the past that you must have regret for those who came before you and it is you who must carry the baggage so that the world does not forget its' past. Unfortunately, we have not perfected memory as an energy, free of regret and negative emotion. This is not limited to a certain segment of society; this is all people across all walks of life. We chose to use this wheel of regret and live in those confines of our society. To run on this wheel and hold these emotions close to our heart for things done decades ago, it is not being done to ensure we do not repeat history, but to silence the eternal child who wants them to love. This is where the concepts of theology started before the love of religion got twisted. It started with a place for support where the luggage could be acknowledged and released. So theologies still practice fasting or confessions to a religious leader as a way to release these regrets and love yourself again.

If you are carrying "generation baggage" that is not yours to carry and was not experienced directly by you, then that baggage can live with you for several lifetimes as you pass it to your offspring. This baggage is a conviction handed to you by those you believed, who provided you love and support, but who told you what to believe based on their perspective…….A single perspective makes you only half blind to what may be the truth. The lion does not regret eating a gazelle, nor does an elephant regret trampling an ant, but man has the memory of an elephant and the ferociousness of the lion if he, his culture, his religion, his politics, his family, his friends, or his football team has been done wrong is some way. We feel a need to have the truth "known".....but, from a single historical perspective. To be clear we are NOT talking about examining the self to understand regret, so one day you can say you live with no regret. It will not be that you will not know regret, it will not be that you wave a magic wand and it disappears, or that you say 10 Hail MARY's and 5 Our Fathers and you and God both get amnesia. It will be that you understand a simple truth. That truth is that the events that occurred where what was most right at the time. People want to go back and change things, "If I could just go back and ...." My response is that if you could go back, if you could be in that same situation all over again, at that time, in that space, you would have done or said exactly the same thing. For that time, in that space it was the most "right" thing. And that "right" thing has brought you to the self-examination you are doing today to give you the opportunity to re-evolve. It has acted as a lesson to be learned, accept it as a lesson, and put the emotion away. We get hit with memories of things we have done and we may say, "I really feel bad about that". There is a negative emotion a person can create the more they think about that event and can soon turn to regret. Instead, if the person says, "That was a good lesson and I have never done that since" or "Wow, yeah that was hard, but I did learn something from the experience". In this way the person is acknowledging the memory, it is not "disappearing", but the negative emotion tied to it can be dismissed. The internal realization here is the goal is not to forget an event, but instead forget the emotion you have tied to it. This is the beauty of forgiveness of the self.

Another great example is the regret of not having spent more time with someone, or choosing a different mate, or a trip not taken. All of this regret is energy better spent thinking about all the adventures you have taken as a result of the path you are on. Again, if you could go back in time and you were exactly who you were at the time, you would have taken the exact same path you are on.

To say, well If I could go back and change things based on what I know now.....Well now that would mean you are two different people and so there is also a good chance that you may not even be presented with the same opportunities. I am waiting for a movie to come out that shows that possibility of being two different people in the same timeline. A movie where the person goes back in time and finds themselves in a completely different place, not even offered the opportunity of fixing the previous mistake, because of the knowledge of self they carried back in time with them. The closest I have seen is called "The Butterfly Effect", but is missing the concept of two people in the same timeline.

There is a 1934 Cartoon many still live to this day. It states, "Forget your history & you're condemned to repeat it". Decades pass before Bob Marley put a twist on it and said, "Don't forget your history nor your destiny." Neither of these quotes mentions anything about regretting your history, living in it, or making your children carry it with them. In fact Mr. Marley is advocating looking to your future while remembering what made you who you are. Memory can carry a lot of regret and can assign a lot of emotions to those memories. Where you are now though, what you are learning while being awake is that you can remember your history, but not tie an emotion to the memory. In this way history is not forgotten, however, regret and negative emotions are not carried by you or sent to future generations. Regret is a lot of noise; it makes it difficult to hear yourself or see your destiny if you decide to anchor yourself to your past. Go and look in the mirror. What you see is your past. So how are you going to change it? Hint….It may start with acknowledging a memory.

Tolerance with the expectations one has for one's self can be harder to accept and recognize than the other types of tolerance. If we begin by being more tolerant with ourselves and being able to recognize where that tolerance exists then we may be able to be tolerant of where the others find themselves drawing lines and voicing their perspectives.

How do you spend the majority of your time "consuming" in this form we call humanity? Is your consuming done with your mind, in books, media, and lectures? Are you consuming this information and then spiting it back out for others to consume as a mass of zombies might? Are you feeding your heart with the intuitive and emotional state it needs to grow or clouding it with emotions like anger and righteousness? Do you focus on being awake through the practice of meditation and feeding your soul with information that will grow the spirit? The key is how do you balance being the mind, the heart, and the eternal child while on this human journey? Overwhelmed? Why I have asked you all these questions all the way along the journey. Have you been consciously reading? You might say I took a page from Gene Rodenberry's book and disguised several concepts of forgiveness throughout the book just under the surface.

Forgiveness is the cure to regret which is the root of many of our physical issues, our relationship issues, and our ability to hear what is in our heart. It's concepts are given to you in piece meal through lectures, inspirational speakers, coaches and in books. This is a small, high potency dose of something that could be written about as a topic all on its own. Once you master how to execute this process it may be you who writes the book and if it is....I hope you send me a copy.

Let's suppose you are on a path which will allow you to move forward with the self- exploration. Now there is an element of forgiveness needed when dealing with regret, but this is not the whole story. Regret is more about acknowledgement and acceptance of things as they have become. What we are taking about with forgiveness is the ability to forget the emotion once tied to the event once you have forgiven it. I know I just quoted a 1934 cartoon saying to forget is to repeat your history, but it is not the event you need to forget, it is the emotion tied to the event.

For example, my wife drives me crazy and in all fairness I drive her crazy. We have our personal challenges with the same things everyone else struggles with and occasionally the stress leads to a disagreement about something REALLY important, like how to load the dishwasher. Now this sounds tame, but our disagreements about the careless loading of the dishwasher have caused tears and hurt feelings on topics unrelated to the dishwasher, but the dishwasher was the instigator of the entire cry fest. We never leave a disagreement to fester, in fact one of us is quick to track down the other in the cases where we leave the room angry. Believe me, an offense as terrible as my carelessly loading the dishwasher has caused me to want to illustrate my masterful use of language in the past.

So here we are a normal couple who love each other and drive each other crazy. We have a disagreement about how to load the dishwasher.....It has been a terrible conversation filled with all kinds of hurtful emotions, on both sides, from a variety of areas that have NOTHING to do with the proper edict for dishwasher loading, but the dishwasher started the whole thing, damn dishwasher! Once we have resolved our issues and talked things out, which can take into the wee hours of the morning, I go downstairs, grab my tools, and remove the dishwasher from the kitchen. Right? I mean the dishwasher was the beginning of it all and this machine caused this terrible "event" to occur. I never want to see this thing again; it will remind me of this terrible emotional state I have just gone through. Silly right? To remove a machine because it reminds us of a hurtful experience. Okay let's say I forgive the dishwasher, but have I truly forgiven the emotions tied to the event? Have I forgiven my spouse? Umm, yes to the second question because she is reading this book. Really, we are quick to forgive those things that do not have feelings, but have a hard time letting go of emotions we tie to those we love. So no I have no emotions towards the dishwasher. So why do we hold emotional baggage of an event after it has been talked through? We will not hold an emotional feeling towards the dishwasher, but many times when something is forgiven the emotions are not forgotten. Emotional forgiveness is critical here, too. The ability to recognize hurt, anger, and frustration in a situation you have told yourself you have already resolved, means this issue is not yet resolved. Fortunately for me, I love my wife and we still have our dishwasher. To hit this point home, I asked my wife what our last fight was about to use it in this book, she thought for a moment and then said, " I don't know….It was probably something stupid." When you forgive, truly forgive, you do not even remember what the emotion was that was tied to the event or what it was really about…..and I have kept all my major appliances in the kitchen where they belong.

People who put themselves in a place where they have to constantly achieve more, reach higher, and run faster are also an excellent example of people who need to forgive themselves, but do not know how. They have set a bar for themselves and if they don't reach it then they have let everyone down. This is the core of what I hear people say. "I let everyone down" is a common theme, then we go back to the original point. Who began to run, who achieved, what did you achieve? Who set the bar higher? Most of the time, it is the individual who set the bar there in the first place. We are told "Reach for the stars", but people forget the second half of this saying and Leo Burnett has a popular version that says, "When you reach for the stars you may not quite get one, but you won't come up with a handful of mud either." A person has not let down "everyone" they have fallen short of reaching their own expectations, which may have been in the stars. So, now that you know your limits will you set the bar lower to make the mark? Will you work harder to reach the goal? Will you still dream about the goal? What is it you are pursuing that has you reaching so high if it is not a part of your bliss?

When you are ready to forgive and love unconditionally you will have evolved passed the vampire stage and you will be able to search within the depths of your heart, the complexity of your mind, and the limitlessness of your higher self to see your connection to everything, not just humanity. You will realize that you are just like everyone else, an essential element that is the greatest part of a whole which lives within all of us and your goals will likely change. Now you are here you are ready to yell it from the mountaintops and exclaim it to everyone " I AM AWAKE", at the top of your lungs. Shhh, remember there are zombies sleeping and vampires waiting to put you back into your place. I know, you can hear the voice, you have learned the art of forgiveness, and have an understanding of unconditional love. Now you want to share it with everyone you know and feel like you are beating your head against a brick wall. You can't watch the evening news anymore and the fear driven society around you is driving you crazy, so what do you do? My advice, remain a seeker. Continue to challenge your understanding of unconditional love. Be able to explain to yourself why in the words of Neale Donald Walsh and his book Conversations with God, "Hitler went to heaven." Ahh, see frustration, anger, opposition of ideas, believe me all really good things at this point. It means you are having conscious thought. How is that thought about Hitler even possible? I know right.

You are awake and ready to tell the world all about it, you want to be awake and face this journey head on!! So here it is. We created all of this. The "boob tube" generation, the X generation, the today. We created it. We allowed our kids to come home to an empty house, allowed the TV or radio to be on Constantly Negative News 24/7 and as a result this is what we created. Now DON"T GO BACK TO SLEEP! That is the easy way. Now you need to start altering your perspective, realize that we have to choose to be our history. We have to want to live in that space, in that way. Instead you want to realize your bliss and understand there can be more than one profound truth. As for Hitler, well the physical form of Hitler ceased to exist, so whatever motivated his heart and mind also died with him. What was left was the eternal child, the eternal child returned to source. This particular ray of light carried with it the noxious tastes of the existence it had during its time with humanity.

I love food. The taste, the texture, the smell. Everything about it! I think what a terrible shame it would be if all I had to eat was what my body "needed". The bland baby mush substance we could feed ourselves to give our body protein. Uck! Now imagine our lives were the same way. No variety, no spice, no noxious tastes that made us cringe. If our lives consisted of all the same lives, same

138

wants, same ambitions, the same desires to drive the same car…Same protein mush…..How boring! If Hitler had listened to himself, he never would have accomplished what he did, if he did not have so many zombies to lead he never would have been successful. If the goals in schools were to relay information about the scared art of unconditional love, we would not have people shooting up schools, theaters, or trying to manipulate humanity by running planes into buildings.

I had a hard time the first time this concept was brought to my attention and part of me still struggles with the idea, but when I examine where that part really is, it is the part of me that exists in my upbringing, in the theology I was taught, and the things I had been told to believe by others. This was not how it rang true to me in other parts of me.

So now you are awake but angry. You can feed off of this anger and approach these topics with fear. Now is when you throw up your hands and yell at me, "Well, Todd what you're saying is we can all do whatever we want and there are no consequences."

Well…..Yes. If our history is not to dictate our future then a resounding "YES!!" This is one future. Consider that our society made up the concept of consequences, didn't we? I know another hornets nest dropped at your feet. Put fear aside for a moment and imagine a world where the universal teaching is one of love, a place where we are listening to our eternal child and have balanced this with the song in our heart and the logic of our minds. Now in that place there would be no desire to be violent, angry, or fearful. We would not need consequences because we would all be pursuing our bliss and part of the trick to unconditional love is the respect we have for ourselves and others. Would there be a need to have consequences then?

I know , I can hear you from the past, THIS IS NOT THE WORLD WE LIVE IN, TODD!! I know, but change one word….Change the word "live" to "lived" and now read your sentence. Can you imagine it? Can you see the people around the world waking up out of their zombie like state and wanting to learn more about the energies that interconnect us? Can you see yourself teaching and learning from the people around you? Stay awake. Be the seeker.

By constantly seeking to teach and be taught those things you need to keep you awake. Amazingly, they will appear with lessons for you to learn and those who are ready to wake up will come to you when you are ready to teach. When the student is ready the teacher will appear. Well, in my mind the teacher and the student can be interchanging roles and neither is perfect. If you are waiting to be in a perfect state before you feel you can teach, you will deprive the world of all you have to offer. This teacher may be a book, a DVD, a friend, a relative, or most importantly....an internal thought. Then you are connected. Then you are awake.

You do not want to go and try to convert the world. Look at our history, remember it. We have already tried that, they were called the Holy Wars, the World Wars, and other conflicts that resulted in terrible losses. Look how well that worked out for humanity, it is time for us to let the opportunities comes to us. We are still dealing with generation baggage. The world will come to you when it is ready and when you are ready. This book was the culmination of thoughts generated over the last ten years. It relays information I have shared and considered for my entire life and I am excited about all of it, however, I will not go out and state a proclamation, preach, or otherwise try to convince someone they need to introduce conflict into their lives. You are still reading this book; you desire the awakened state. You are hearing the voice inside you and it is encouraging you to keep reading. To you this is real, so make it real to yourself and let others find what is real to them....That is evolution. Going out and starting a new form of theology or school of thought is doing little to move humanity forward. Instead allow those who are interested seek you out AND challenge you. This is a part of paying it forward and is something we all enjoy doing, once we are ready to teach what we know AND learn what we are to be taught.

Looking for a way to break the cycle? Talk to Juan Mann, whose mission was to reach out to others and offer them.....a hug. This campaign to share a hug with a fellow human being led to a "ban" on hugs.....True story. Another Internet search opportunity for you here, if you are not familiar with the story. He has changed people's lives by offering them a connection with another human being during their, otherwise, chaotic day. A man standing in the middle of a pedestrian mall with a sign that says, "Free Hugs", inspires me. It tells me that not only are people waking up, but others are offering themselves unconditionally to aid in that process. I find it interesting that so many people have received so much from a hug. Not only that, but here is a question for you. Who receives more from the hug? The Hugger? Or the huggie? Or could it be that they both receive something from the experience?

The Black Eyed Peas have a song titled " One Tribe" and it is profound when you listen to the words. Phrases like "let's all catch amnesia", and "all that evil that they feed ya". Why would a government put a ban on hugs? Why should people need to sign a petition to get that decision reversed? How is it that we allowed governments to have this much power over not only our livelihoods, but also our person? We start with forgiveness.

The way we become "One" is to start with forgiveness. This forgiveness eventually gets to those in our physical world, but first we have to start with ourselves. This is important because of what I put you through in the last chapter and what we have been through in our lives.

First, we came into this world as beautiful little vampires who understood nothing of their physical form and only understood love. We needed and relied on the love and caring nature of others for the first several months. We were introduced to unconditional love through our parents and relied on them to teach us how to manifest things within our environment. Then we learned that love had conditions based on what society had taught our parents, mentors, and guides. Then we were introduced to mass media, taught how to use it in school. We were then further educated by the institutions and society's we, as a people, have allowed to be built around us. Through our culture and society we learned terms like ego, fear, and regret. Then we topped off our education with being inundated with the concepts and views of politics, religion, and success.

Many of us adapted to the rules of our society and became skilled at "fitting in" which, for many, required turning things off inside of us. This is similar to first grade where everyone put their head down on their desk for 20 minutes to take a nap....Unfortunately, many adults became overwhelmed by their education, have left their heads on the desk, and turned into societies zombies.

For others we learned to use our skills and understanding of energy to manipulate energy and situations to better our position within the society we were introduced into. The child vampire has grown to adulthood and now can feed off of situations and society with relative ease. In this case, though, the feeding is occurring at the expense of others.

Based on the expectations of society you should now feel regret for this action, or maybe anger at someone for doing this "to you", or maybe anger towards me for telling such heinous lies that fly in the face of everything you have been taught to believe. The end result could be you needing to return to your previous vampire or zombie state. Those who do are well trained.....For the rest of you.....The final step is the most trying and most glorious of them all. It is forgiveness, but it is forgiveness of self. Trying to forgive others is a sellout tactic many people try and use to better position themselves and avoid the root issue. It starts with your history, your baggage. Why does this "event" make you feel the emotions you feel? Have you been hurt this way before? Have you done this to someone else? Why do you feel you need to forgive another? Or why do you feel you need to be ashamed for a certain action?

PAY IT FORWARD

To understand creation of our pain and suffering starts and ends with us is an amazing concept to comprehend. So how do you pay this forward?

When you see people dressed as "Gothic" this is a social statement to the world about what they enjoy about their culture. This has been newly created subculture seen flourish in the last 20 years and it has always intrigued me. I was excited when I had the opportunity to ask a young lady why the colors were so appealing to her and what it meant to her to dress as she did. At first she seemed put off until she realized I was sincerely interested. She explained to me that it was a fashion statement for her. I asked her what the "fashion statement" was she was trying to get across. " She said that this was how she told the world she did not care what they thought that she was her own person." We continued our conversation and talked about her need for impact in her life, on her life, and how that was significant to others….not to get attention, but feeling significant in her world. We discovered, together, many things during our conversation. My blood ran cold when she looked at me and said "Well, how I dress is really how I feel inside, dead." I suddenly felt responsible, yet this was not my child and I had only just met her an hour ago. That feeling was my challenge and I had to resist the urge to "tell her" what she needed to discover for herself. You see she gave me the opportunity to be the student and hear her journey, but I could have easily taken control and told her my perspective. She helped me understand that I helped create every culture and subculture we see in our society today. When we walk down the street and shake our head in disbelief at what young people are wearing….or half wearing….We had a hand in creating through our attention to our "One tribe" of humanity. Now it is possible to get emotional and say, "that is not my mess" or "I cannot be accountable for that".

In the case of my beautiful friend she discovered she was using "shock and awe" to relate a message to her family and the world that was one of being lost inside herself. What a beautiful young lady to have the courage to express herself for others to see she felt disconnected. Her message was not one of rebellion, or one of needing help, it was just one of her evolution. The message was just getting lost in herself to the point where she could not hear it anymore. In my mind, she did not want to go to sleep, so she was fighting so hard for a vampire identity that she could sustain. Soon we discovered her anger with herself and what was needed for her to forgive herself and then move that forgiveness out into her world. It was an honor to have learned from her.

You are on this same journey and it is an inspired one. It is getting to the root of your issues that is the key and many times this has nothing to do with an event you want to blame everything on. This is where having family, a true friend, or a trusted professional coach/therapist can help. All of these people are masters at hearing your eternal child slip words out in your conversation that you completely miss. They can hear your inner self speaking through your words and know what the next question should be or next comment should include. So many people are anxious about paying someone to listen to them, but understand that the good ones.....they not only listen to your words, but connect with you during your journey. They hear what is going on past what you want them to hear and the true guides you bring into your life will help you see what it is you are truly saying.....Even if you don't really want to hear it. This can take some time so be kind to yourself through the process.

When I was in high school, hazing freshman was a common and expected occurrence. Putting freshman in trash cans and rolling them down the hill or giving them a wedgie. For those of you not familiar with this wonderful tradition it would involve high school juniors and seniors grabbing a freshman boy, pulling them to the back of the bus and pulling their underwear, up until the elastic band separated and they would pull that up over your head and wear it on their head for the remainder of the 45 minute bus ride home. Yes, I said catholic school.

I myself was not a recipient of this hazing, thanks to a neighbor friend who was a senior and convinced the ringleader to spare me. All he wanted from me in return was a handshake. Something I still remember having a very hard time doing.

Now a decade later, when I was seeking through my Reiki Master training. I had a young gentleman who came to me and was suffering from cancer. His father was adamant about finding an alternative to chemo. I had agreed to work with the young man as long as he was still seeing a physician. This young man had a lot of trauma in his life and we spent three times a week working together. The spots in his lungs began to disappear and his blood work was "almost normal". Then the father said he needed to take his son out of state, that there was a disagreement in treatment approaches between the parents. I found out six months later that the young man had passed away. In the hours after I got this news it was those high school hazing memories that came rushing back to me and I realized the anger I still had surrounding these hazing events, but the hazing had not happen to me, so I tried to let it go. Then I started to dig at the real issue and discovered that I was even more frustrated about the helplessness at not being able to do anything to stop the hazing of my friends, so I had moved my forgiveness of self from anger, to regret. I thought I had identified the root of my energy and began trying to heal, but became even more frustrated. What had wrapped me up so much that this old baggage would resurface at the news of this young man's passing? I understood the helplessness aspect and had learned how to acknowledge the event and release it, but it still nagged at me, I had not yet gotten to the root of this energy, this baggage.

It took me almost a week to get to the root of this problem. You see it turns out that at the end of my Sophomore year I had been riding this same bus for two years and our high school busing service also carted kids from a naval "prep school". This prep school had required a dress code resembling a naval dress uniform, which made these kids stand out even more. One of these kids was obnoxious and viewed himself as better than most (my perspective) and since a ban had been placed on all hazing that year he felt entitled to be even more obnoxious. One day he got unbearable with several people on the bus ride home and he and I exchanged words about his attitude. He basically told me to deal with it, since there was no more hazing allowed. I told him my friends and I would see him at his bus stop at the end of the school year which was less than 6 weeks away. This was when I started driving instead of riding the bus. He continued to carry on and fueled the fire for a couple weeks. On the last day of school, I was headed home and was asked to drop off a classmate who lived on the same road as the obnoxious youth. I had forgotten all about my idle threat. I knew the bus was minutes behind us, so I pulled over to wait for this kid and was set on fulfilling my promise to adjust his attitude.

My classmate talked to me and found that part of me that was past the negative emotions I was harboring for this kid. I started to relive my freshman year and experience that helplessness all over again.....Something I was about to do to someone else..... I realized I was about to become "one of those guys", the guys I hated. I took my friend home and as we were leaving the neighborhood the bus dropped off the young man I had been angry with. He looked very nervous, had no obnoxious words, and I felt his helplessness as we drove by him. That feeling of helplessness revitalized in me when I was not able to help the cancer patient beat his disease. It had ignited unresolved baggage I had been carrying around about bullies in high school who I had shaken hands with right before they grabbed another freshman and pulled them to the back of the bus, making me feel helpless. The helplessness I felt for the event with the cancer patient was just masking the root issue that caused this frustration to continue and resurface. I had been carrying around regret about a young man who I had made feel helpless. I never acknowledged it and I never dealt with it. It then manifested itself almost 20 years later and I could not identify the issue for over a week.

So it sounds easy to open yourself up to others experiences and allow them to be your teacher, however, this one event had several "roots" I had to work through. Once I could hear my eternal child many things started to be resolved within myself. This is where you must have courage because when you look into the mirror of your heart the reflection of what you see can be harsh unresolved truths. For me, in this example, once I understood it, I could forgive myself for not stepping up and defending friends when I was a freshman, I could forgive myself for almost becoming someone I did not want to become. By realizing the root of these emotions I have been able to release the emotional regret around those events which triggered all of this emotional "soup".

I thought I was dealing with one thing related to the passing of this young man, but it was being rooted by another event or baggage; I had not thought of for decades. Amazing how that baggage just lingers within us, isn't it? Amazing how our greatest teachers may be the children on the playground or a teenage cancer patient, isn't it?

Now imagine a time and space where every man, woman, and child have the capacity to be in this same space of thought. This is the concept of us all being one tribe, humanity's eternal child. This points to why we need to forgive self, first. If we can forgive ourselves and love ourselves unconditionally, then society will right its course automatically. Our best way to help society and everything else we support, is to start paying it forward by fixing ourselves. By doing this we will have students and teachers enter our lives as we need them, be able to consciously examine each event, and will quickly identify the voice of our eternal child; making it impossible for us to wrong anyone else. Right now we justify our daze, or our vampire traits by watching the world act as infants and determine that if it is ok for everyone else to do it, then why can't I. I applaud you for not wanting to be one of the masses.

It is a shame that for many of us the only time we awaken and truly appreciate our humanity is through tragedy. Consider for a moment that there is no soul on this earth who prays harder for peace, then a soldier. A soldier sees the greatest atrocities one man can bestow on another. To be asked by your country to take a life is to ignore your humanity, then to be congratulated for it, given a medal, and being told it is appreciated by others in the society that you have taken another life, is an internal struggle none of us should have to endure. Yet this sense of self-worth does nothing for the regret or disconnection the soldier has suffered. They put their humanity in a box and many of them cannot find that box to let it back out or have found that box, but are more scared of the self-judgment that lies within the box then they would be going back into combat. They lost the voice of that eternal child and now know they stand in judgment of themselves because society has "lost its' mind". Unfortunately, our culture and humanity today only re-evolves through experiences and some of the most horrific experiences. The results are some of the most profound opportunities for re-evolutions of society's, cultures, and self. An example of this is the events that occurred on September 11 when there was a significant loss of life. These were some of the brightest hours for humanity because of the incredible support that came from around the world during that tragedy. This did not diminish the significance of the loss of life or those affected by this tragedy, however, this brought people together for a higher purpose and these people came from all walks of life from all over the country and around the world to aid other humans during this trying time. This moment of humanity created a revolution of self, but also offered an equal and opposite reaction. Our society's had the opportunity to instill fear in the masses, as well. This fear had geopolitical impacts, religious impact and personal impacts. If we were awake we had the opportunity to see both the positive and negative impacts. What would you say our society chose to focus on? What did our mainstream media focus on?

There are a lot of groups out there today trying to re-evolve these institutions of government and they are known as activist, tree huggers, and sometimes even hackers. All of these people have woken up and know what they do not like about the world, but what do they know about themselves? The problem is most of these groups are led by vampires who will tell the people what it is they want to hear or need to hear to feel they're a valuable part of that particular movement.

The power Anonymous has used to illustrate the power of the Internet versus the power of mass media has been a great social experiment. On one side you have those using the Internet, through a group of people who are not tied to the social norm and have no desire to be a part of the society as it stands today, has spent much of their time in the virtual world of the Internet as kids and never really had much use for the social norms. This group, while they may be classified as outcasts by some, are considered Superheroes by those they have helped globally. This group did something no TV, radio, or newspaper was able to accomplish. This group assisted entire countries with changing their leadership. While mass media reported and vilified the group, the group (without leadership) helped a country change its' leadership.

As with any group this group has some radicals involved with the operations which leave the methods used questionable, however, this group is evolutionary and the people in it are looking for a greater part of themselves to be represented. This group is showing how technology can aid in that effort. Now before you take pen to paper and send me proof of the evils of the group, let me save you some time. I spent 10 years in the computer security profession. I know what they have been accused of, however, I also took the time to reach beyond the media. While many of these posts are shocking I believe this is one way for a person to get shocked into reality. So this group is looked at as deviant or people without a moral compass, however, when looking at what they have done for the greater good it is hard to argue that they, as a group, have done less good for people then have done harm to people. I do not agree with their tactics or methods in respect to some of the things that they are trying to accomplish, as I stated before the solution starts with yourself, but until we are ready to face that we will continue to create cultures like this who will be in our face and force us to re-evolve. This is not true of the mass media institution they have definitely, as a group, have caused more fear and done more harm to the masses then they have helped the masses of society.

I always thought it would be an interesting classroom assignment to write a description of the people of earth for a visiting alien race. My description has changed over the years based on my experiences, but here is what I have to date. If asked to record a brief intro about the people of earth for an alien race to describe humanity it would be like this:

We the people of earth are all made of the same genetic goo (yes goo is a very technical description here on earth). We all use relatively the same mental capacity and have the same lifespan. However, we have different views, different beliefs, and different values systems based on the color of our skin, where we live in the world, and capacity to evolve our cultural systems. We have built cultures and society's that make it appropriate to hurt each other based on these differing views and use our creative nature to create financial systems that are balanced so that less than 10% of the world experiences wealth. We feed this financial system with war to gain resources others have, and may either cause or ignore genocide. Understand that humanity is like a young child, it can be as kind as it is cruel and not be able to explain why. The race has not yet evolved past infancy of understanding itself. It still focuses on the manipulation of the physical world and the consumption of its finite resources. I would not recommend visiting this tiny planet for some time yet as the fate humanity has determined for itself, is still unknown. It will either allow itself to be consumed by violence and fear or it will evolve to acceptance through unconditional love. To date the majority has yet to decide and remains asleep.

So at the end of this book you realize you are exactly where you should be on your journey. As a mentor, I have asked you the appropriate questions and provided very few perspectives. By now you have realized that it is your perspective that must be addressed and that you have all those answers inside of you, if you can just hear yourself. You have the incredible power to heal and forgive your past of regret and negative emotions, manifest your brilliant future, and have it within you to aid others on their journey to do the same. I know this about you because you have made it this far. All it takes is your courage to walk in the dark as we turn the lights up together for humanity.

I will not be surprised if I am walking through a park one day and there is a person sitting on a park bench with a sign that says, "Free Friend". It will be a great day when we can re evolve and look at each other as the student and the teacher, the hugger and the hugged. There are other great adventures to explore, but for now I appreciate you accompanying me on this one. Namaste'

Remember to Love Courageously, Live Boldly, and Listen Consciously every day.

EXTRAS

This section is designed as a reference to capture all the movies and books mentioned in the book. This is a reference of sorts for you so you do not have to search back through the book to find a particular movie discussed or book mentioned.

- Seven minutes of movie wisdom:
  https://www.youtube.com/watch?v=n8CaC4RMwsM
- Babies require human contact-
  http://www.livestrong.com/article/72120-effect-human-contact-newborn-babies/
- Part of a lost Generation by J. Reed
  https://www.youtube.com/watch?v=KAt2v-XIfJk
- Book by Joseph Campbell titled "The Power of Myth"
- George Lucas movie titled "Star Wars"
- Movie titled "The Matrix"
  https://www.youtube.com/watch?v=zE7PKRjrid4&list=PL842063FF9CD2577F
  https://www.youtube.com/watch?v=O4yuhvccQog&list=PL842063FF9CD2577F
- "With Honors"
  https://www.youtube.com/watch?v=h9ZiluviVVs
- "The Truman Show"
  https://www.youtube.com/watch?v=NkZM2oWcleM
- "Liar, Liar"
  https://www.youtube.com/watch?v=dAE7uOO_4v4
- "Avatar" https://www.youtube.com/watch?v=cRdxXPV9GNQ
- Book by Neil Donald Walsh titled "Conversations with God"
  https://www.youtube.com/watch?v=M0eGkQFXIOQ
- Bill Cosby titled "Bill Cosby Himself"
  https://www.youtube.com/watch?v=qyMSc97UksM
- DVD called "What the Bleep"
- DVD called "The Secret"
- Tom Shadyac DVD called "I Am"- Institute of HeartMath-
  http://www.heartmath.org/research/research-publications/electrophysiological-evidence-of-intuition-part-1-the-surprising-role-of-the-heart.html
- "The Matrix" fans "There is no spoon."
  https://www.youtube.com/watch?v=dzm8kTlj_0M
- Movie called "The Dead Poet's Society"
  https://www.youtube.com/watch?v=w8fu-hq3S7A
- Movie called "The Wizard of Oz" 1939

- Movie called "The Butterfly Effect"

This section provides ideas or "steps" used to create the book. These were some of the key concepts used when manifesting what you are reading.

What can I do if I discover I am a zombie?

If you are a zombie and have been reading this book, then you have taken a journey where you should realize you are not a zombie. A zombie would not have made it through the frustration, anger, or fear to have comprehended this much of the book, but let's say you started as a zombie. Now what?

- Go on with the status quo. Steps for a zombie always have to include the option to stay right where you are. It is not satisfying, but it may be safe…. OR!!
- Start with quiet contemplation…This is not meditation, really. It is moments of disconnect from others. Leave your phone on the desk and go for a walk.
- Do not eat your lunch at your desk. Make yourself move into another, less hectic space, for lunch.
- Stare…..It is time to really look at yourself in the mirror. See who you were and appreciate that the image you see is who you were….Not who you are today

What if I discover I am a vampire?

Be kind to yourself and remember that you are no different than you were as a newborn. You have never outgrown the idea of feeding off of others and so these steps are designed to wean you away from the need to use others.

- The desire to "share" your thoughts and perspective will drive you to feel the need to share. Resist this and instead focus on listening to another perspective. Your perspective will still be there when you get finished listening.
- When you anger or become negative in a conversation, they have won. You cannot listen or see when clouded by negative emotions. Ask yourself why you are feeling these emotions.
- Disconnect from the mass media world. Start with a couple nights a week and then a couple weeks a month. You will find with time, the only thing you are truly missing is the negativity.

I cannot get past being a dark walker!

- Appreciate and have gratitude for being in this seeker state of being
- Find ways to harmonize with the elements and people around you
    - I start my day by repeating one of two words as I do my morning routine. My words are either harmony or gratitude. In the evening as I prepare for bed I will repeat the other of the two words. It calms my mind.

CREDITS:

Thank you to the following
contributors:

Editing: Jackie Olsen

Illustrations: Shawn Borandi

Photo Cover: Trista Borandi

My amazing family and friends
who supported this effort from
the beginning.

My best friend and wife
Christy, who I love passionately
and who still; holds both my
hand and heart .

In true movie fashion, this is the "after credits" clip often seen in movies to keep you around until the very end of the movie. I am not excited about this movie ending, so when I started wrapping this up I thought I would add something I have been carrying around since I was a teenager.

When I saw 14 years old I was awakened in the middle of the night from a dream that seemed so real. I sat up and took pen to paper to capture as much of the dream as I could, no computers back then and my cursive was awful! I carried this with me all these years knowing one day I would see it published.

So, from the eternal child of a 14 year old boy who was struggling to find his way in this world. This is what was manifested into his reality about life. It called itself, the journeys end.

The Journeys End

I walked with a bounce in my step and anticipation in my heart, wondering what I was going to find in the painting. I approached the summit of the hill with an enthusiasm I had not felt for a decade... I recall the story as if it was yesterday.

It was 10 years ago, when I traveled great distances on my small limbs. I was barely old enough to see over the hay growing in the field. While looking out over these hay fields I noticed a grassy knoll and recognized several overgrown paths leading off in different directions. One of these paths lead off to the north where I would lay by the river on a warm summer's day. The trail intersecting it leading off to the east passes a tree that allowed me to climb high enough to see the whole world and touch the sky. There was yet another path that led to the field where I would race the wind; running so fast that I could hear the wind in my years trying to keep up with me.

My favorite of these narrow dusty trails is the one that I am walking today. In the distance I can now see a weather-beaten shack from the rich foliage that covers the entire valley. A smile stretches across my face as I recall the day I found "my castle" and made a lifelong friend.

On that day it was nearing the season of snow and all the rich foliage had turned colors or fallen from the trees allowing me to see more than I would see on a summer's day. I had recently turned 10 years old and was determined to make it to the top of the summit before the first snowfall, so that I could overlook the valley, stare down at my house, but most importantly to see what was on the other side of the hill. On that day I had traveled further than ever before and was fascinated by what kind of treasure lay beyond the top of that hill. As I reached the summit and looked down into the valley with wonder and amazement as I could cover my whole house by closing one eye and putting my thumb over the house. I took in all the brilliant colors of the changing season and stared at the outlines of the many paths of my life.

While surveying the dazzling region of paradise I had become so familiar with I noticed something new among the landscape. It was something I had never seen before. I had not traveled so far or were so high and in the summer months it would be well disguised by the rich green leaves on the nearby trees. I was so taken by this new discovery that I spent no time looking at what lay beyond the summit of that hill, but instead moved closer to what appeared to be an old shack. As I drew closer I could see the frame of this old shack much clearer and I became excited because now I would have a place to call my own and this would be… My castle!

The secret place that has been waiting for me for a long time as I approached my new treasure I became increasingly excited and moved faster and faster towards the front door. Boldly throwing open the door I claim my prize and discovered that my castle came equipped with an old wooden chair of bed and a stove. It was then that I became completely distracted by the true treasure of my castle. There hung on the wall was a picture of masterful color and expression. It was full of life and I was drawn closer to study it. I was completely drawn into the painting because the colors seem to come alive and move and create new forms. They were moving on the canvas in an almost synchronized fashion coming together blending to create a familiar scene. Soon the scene I was staring at was that of me running through the hay fields racing the wind. I was surprised to see similar paintings on two of the adjoining walls. They seem to come alive as I looked at each in turn and I found that the paintings each became the scene of a certain precious memories in my life. As I moved to the next painting and the colors began to blend I saw my house which was sitting amongst a river of grass, then moving to the other painting I watched as the colors haphazardly rearrange themselves on the canvas to form the spot of the river where I caught my first fish.

Suddenly a voice asked, "What do you see?" As I was suddenly pulled away from the world of painting and found myself once again standing in my castle. The warm and quiet voice inquired the second time "Don't stop, what do you see?" Out of the doorway shadow came an old lady short in stature but with eyes of a newborn and a smile that warmed my very being. I had been startled and became defensive with this woman who had just barged into my castle without even knocking. Without thinking and with my heart still racing in my throat I snapped back "My River of course. Now, what are you doing in my castle?!"

She seemed to glide towards the painting I was looking at and as if in a trance she replied "Well, I guess I am the keeper of this castle. What part of the river do you see in this painting?" I remember now that this must have been a funny sight for her to return home and see this scrawny 10-year-old child insisting that I did not need a keeper for the castle and recall she just smiled and continued to stare at the painting waiting for me to answer her questions. I recall being annoyed because I had not invited her in and did not know who she was, so instead of answering her question I asked her what she saw in the painting. It was then that she turned towards me with a fire in her eyes and a smile on her face and said an almost a secret whisper one word "life" . As this word passed her lips it burns my ears as we locked eyes for the first time and suddenly I wasn't afraid because she felt familiar in some way. When I broke eye contact she simply moved to the next painting and again wanted to know what it was that I saw. She simply smiled and asked me questions about the details of the painting, but seemed to understand and appreciate what I saw, never telling me I was wrong.

Days turned into weeks and weeks became months as I would visit my castle and spend time with its keeper every chance I got in those youthful days. As the months became years it was not so easy to find time to visit my castle. During the years I visited my castle and spoke with "the keeper", a nickname that stuck and became a joke between us. During these times I would tell her of my races against the wind, the trees that reach the sky, and other exciting adventures I undertook with each passing year.

As it was on the first day she would listen tentatively and with genuine interest in specific details about what it was I saw in the paintings. One day, the keeper invited me to go with her to a gallery. As we walked back to the castle I asked her why it was paintings changed when I came to visit and I did not see the same scene every time. As with every lesson she taught she stopped looked me in the eye and replied simply "the paintings are the same, it is you that has changed." I remember being genuinely confused, as the keeper put her arm around me and we continue down the path I asked, "why is it that the gallery paintings never change?" The keeper thought for a moment and then said the gallery paintings are an expression of life through another person's perspective and are set in the oils on the canvas. What you see in those paintings at your castle is life the way you perceive it as it changes and you grow. The painting pulls you into it, involves your very being, and creates a masterpiece complete with your perceptions and experiences. It is your journey as your inner self enjoys your life. This is why you will only see your most cherished moments within these paintings.

As years wore on I remembered these lessons less and less and after four years the visits to my castle became less frequent and the oils on the canvas of the painting seem to flow less easily and scenes seemed to repeat or not form at all. By the time I had reached 16 years old it took concentration for me to get the oils on the canvas to move or for any forms to take shape. I would make up stories of what I saw in the paintings or tell old stories and began to wonder if it every really moved at all. On top of this I remember talking with school friends about the lady in the cabin and their perspective was that she was crazy. I started to wonder this myself. In all these years she only had three paintings one on each wall with an obvious empty space on the fourth wall as if she was still looking for the fourth painting. On my last visit I remember asking her why she did not sell the painting so she could earn enough money to move into town and not live in this broken down cabin any longer. She simply smiled as she had always done looked me in the eyes and said "I enjoy being the keeper of this castle and I cannot sell a life that is borrowed for a brief time, I can only enjoy the brilliance of it while I have it. Many of these words that she shared with me made no sense and I became more afraid than I was when I was 10 years old. Now I had friends who were telling me that she might be crazy and this caused conflict within me.

As time progressed I would travel all the trails less often and I began creating some new ones. Soon I would only travel the trail to my castle for holidays and birthdays. Soon all the dusty trails began to fade with new trails being cut.

The keeper was always happy to see me and was always interested in what I saw on her paintings. I asked her once last week why she had not, in all these years, bought a fourth painting. She just gave me her warm smile I had grown so accustomed to over the years and said, "If the painting is constantly changing in your mind's eye, why would we need more than that which we have experienced and can comprehend about our journey?"

She never in these 10 years bought another painting, until today. I was with some friends in town and I saw her leaving the gallery. Under her arm she was awkwardly maneuvering a large brown enveloped frame. I ran across the plaza to intercept her and inquire about the rare find. What is it I asked enthusiastically. She looked at me and just smiled that smile. I smiled in return and I understood my blunder. The bond had grown stronger between us so it was a wordless knowledge that we shared she knew I was eager to see it and invited me to visit the castle. With that she smiled warmly and started her journey home. I wanted to go with her, however, my journey carried me in opposite direction, for the moment. I said to her as she walked away "I will see you soon keeper". She turned and smiled and continued on her way down her path.

All of those wonderful memories bring me to this point and for the first time in 10 years I find myself knocking on the castle door waiting for the keeper to open it for me. I was brimming with excitement and anticipation, but there was no response no one opened the door. I slowly opened the door and moved into the center of the small room that once seemed so massive. There on the once empty wall was the new painting and I move towards it. It was strange because I felt no pull or drawing force from this painting. I looked at it intentionally for several moments, but it was a motionless painting like one I have seen in the gallery hundreds of times before. The painting had a peaceful quality to it; however, the brilliant colors did not move or organize themselves at all for me. I could not see anything in this painting and recalled what the keeper had said about perspective. I became frustrated, like a 10 year old child, and was confused as to why the keeper would buy it. In fact, I wanted to tear it off the wall and do away with the painting altogether, but instead turned away from it and began to leave.

This is when I noticed the keeper lying silently on the bed staring at the picture. When I noticed her lying there I began to share my feelings of disappointment with this painting. As I approached I realize the familiar warmth of her smile in the fire in her eyes were both extinguished. I looked back at the painting as tears began to stroll down my cheeks and I realized that the last lesson taught to me by the keeper of the castle was that life's journey can be represented in the same manner and perspective as the journey's end.

Zombie Fact Sheet

Description: These people are those who are not awake. Many have no desire to be awake and those who are awake may cringe when I use a zombie as the label to describe the "UNAWAKE". I could call you a virus, but that was used in the movie "The Matrix", besides Hollywood has popularized the idea of human beings who do things without thought while consuming everything they can get their hands on. Zombies move in massive groups of people, as a general rule this can be looked at as a daily occurrence in those societies where everything is disposable or has a one year cycle before a newer one comes out. The zombies buy new products, consume resources and throw them away as quickly as they can afford to buy a newer version of the same product. The majority of this mass is kept relatively happy by the vampires and in a state of relative comfort to avoid a zombie apocalypse.

Meal preferences: Fast food, something that will take minutes where social interaction can be limited. Zombies may eat together, but they are on their phones, listening to their music, or carry only limited conversations with each other.

Manner of Dress: Depends on what the job requires or social agenda dictates. They are very interested in being a part of the crowd.

Music Preferences: Heavy, angry, mind numbing, or music with negative emotions to feed off of are most popular types of music for the zombie. A heavy bass sound and low vibrational tones are most comforting.

Movie Preferences: Action movies that do not require thought, Comedy and romance are ok if they lead the audience and do not require any thought of plot or reason why.

Other entertainment: Video games are very popular with this culture. Many of the games are violent, have an easy to follow story and focus on the action.

Feeding the soul: They prefer to feed off of others, by being a part of a group that laughs or teases at another's expense, so they move in packs to maintain their strength. At times when no other worthy target is around, they feed on the energies of each other.

Vampire Fact sheet

Description: They do not rely on big groups for strength; they have mastered the art of feeding off the masses and have stepped up one level in the re-evolutionary chain. They lead businesses, societies, and governments; they run institutions and know how to keep a balance to the society needs and wants. Like in the movies there are good vampires......and bad vampires but considering we all start as vampires when we are newborns......This is where we start our journey with the options of sliding backwards into a dazed zombie state, or forward into an awakened state of being.

Meal preferences: A slow enjoyable meal is preferred. The dining can take hours and in that time the discussions are filled with nothing meaningful, except to those who understand the art of small talk and strategic conversations.

Manner of Dress: "Dress to Impress" is the order of the day. Sharp dressed in a "power suit" to let everyone see them coming and know they are important. BE aware the vampire is very keen on fitting in as well. They will know how to change their manner of dress to fit into the occasion. They may not just look comfortable doing it, they will miss their "power clothes" and most of the time when trying to fit in, the clothes will be brand new.

Music Preferences: Familiar with all forms of classical music more out of necessity than enjoyment. Able to move between musical preferences and may span a wide variety of interests in order to remain fluid in any conversation or while feeding in any environment.

Movie Preferences: The more emotionally moving the better. Vampires feed off of the energy of others while they are emotionally charged. A vampire enjoys movies and will walk out of theater completely charged up, even if the movie was on a sober topic.

Other entertainment: Sporting events of all types, but not if alone. The vampire prefers to be at an event where they can be surrounded by others during the event. Again the emotional enhancement of a live sporting event charges the "batteries" to full capacity.

Feeding the soul: They feed off of the zombies, they feed off of any emotionally charged situation, and know how to use the energy to their advantage. They can take any negative situation and turn it to their advantage and know how to manipulate situations with mastery.

www.ingramcontent.com/pod-product-compliance
Lightning Source LLC
Chambersburg PA
CBHW061724020426
42331CB00006B/1089